AF264340

Poets and Poems of The New South

Volume II

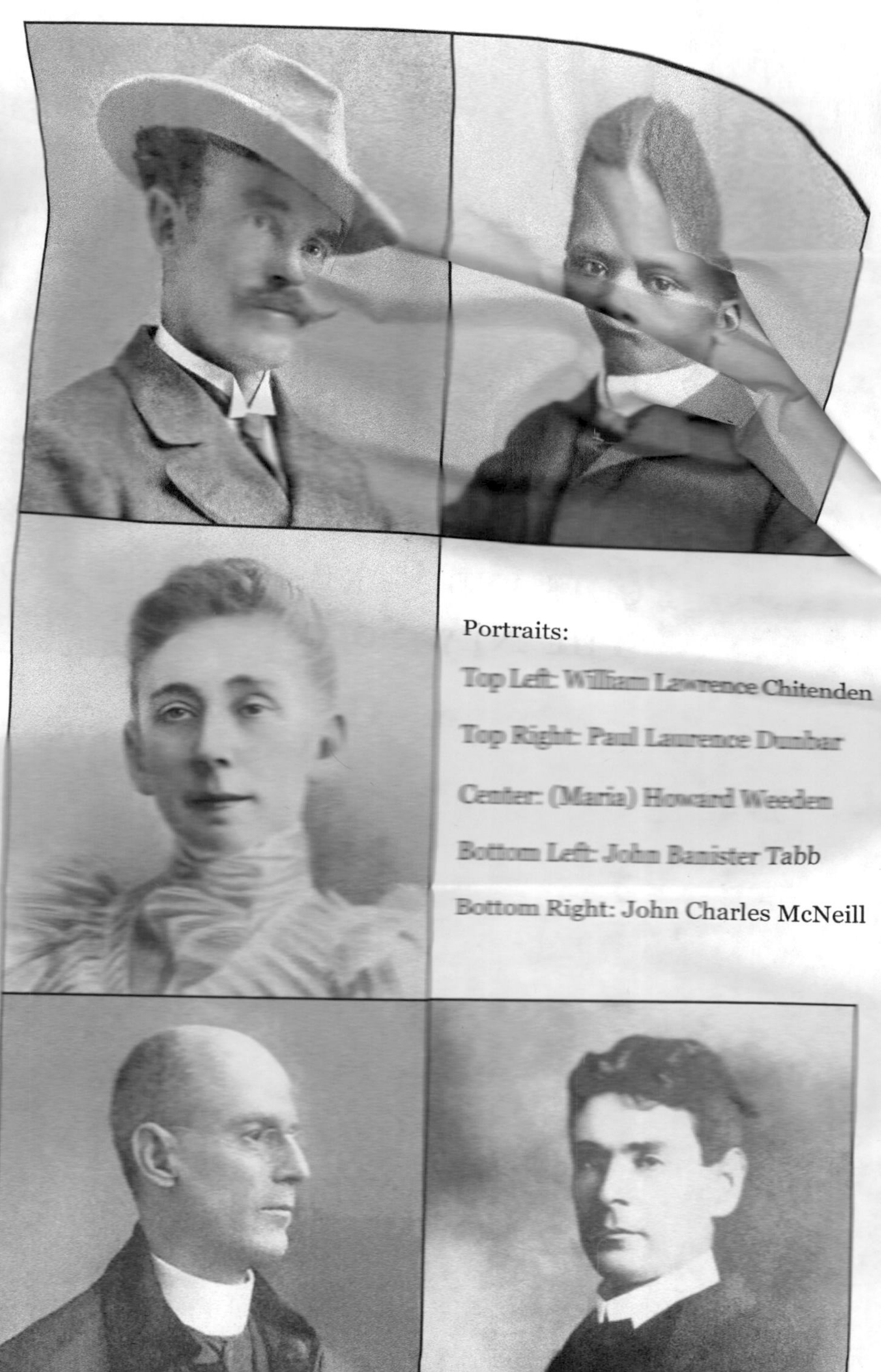

Portraits:

Top Left: William Lawrence Chitenden

Top Right: Paul Laurence Dunbar

Center: (Maria) Howard Weeden

Bottom Left: John Banister Tabb

Bottom Right: John Charles McNeill

The Land They Loved:

Volume V

POETS AND POEMS OF THE NEW SOUTH

Volume II

Edited by

Clyde N. Wilson

The Land They Loved Volume V:
Poets and Poems of The New South, Volume 2

Produced in the Republic of South Carolina by

SHOTWELL PUBLISHING LLC

Post Office Box 2592

Columbia, So. Carolina 29202

www.ShotwellPublishing.com

Cover design: Boo Jackson. All portraits are public domain.

ISBN: 978-1-963506-64-8

FIRST EDITION

10 9 8 7 6 5 4 3 2 1

Contents

Foreword, xi

Memory

J. E. Bataile
Dedication of the Monument to the Defenders of Vicksburg, 1

Virginia Frazer Boyle
The Wizard of the Saddle, 3

Josie Frazee Cappleman
The Old Time Darky, 6

Edward Ward Carmack
The South..., 9

William Lawrence Chitenden
"Remember The Alamo", 10
My Old Friend, "The Majah Green", 12
Old Fort Phantom Hill, 15

Columbus Drew
Dedication of the Soldiers' Monument Tallahassee. 1880, 17
The Prayer of Milo Cooper, 19

Paul Laurence Dunbar
Chrismus On the Plantation, 21
After A Visit, 23

Armistead Churchill Gordon
The Little Old Church, 25

Clifford Anderson Lanier
The First Confederate White House, 29

Carlyle McKinley
At Timrod's Grave, 30

John Trotwood Moore
Sam Davis, 33

Clarence N. Ousley
When the Mint is in the Liquor, 36

Thomas Nelson Page
Uncle Gabe's White Folks, 37

Cale Young Rice
Daniel Boone's Last Look Westward, 38

Gilbert Moxley Sorrell
(From his memoirs, on Lee), 41

Zula Camille Vaughan
"Dixie", 42

(Maria) Howard Weeden
The Banjo of the Past, 44
Beaten Biscuit, 45

The Worst of War, 46

A Voice of the Night, 47

Mother and Mammy, 48

The Old Boatman, 49

When Manners Were in Bloom, 50

Faith

MARY BAYARD DEVEREUX CLARKE

John Wesley's Foot-Print, 53

Matter, 55

The Happy Valley, 57

Thoughts, 59

GO DOWN, MOSES, *60*

HILTON ROSS GREER

A Prairie Prayer, 61

JOEL CHANDLER HARRIS

Revival Hymn, 64

CHARLES WILLIAM HUBNER

To a Mocking Bird, 66

WILLIAM PRESTON JOHNSTON

Creation, 68

SWING LOW, SWEET CHARIOT, *71*

JOHN BANISTER TABB

Evolution, 74

Kildee, 75

LEONARD CHARLES VAN OPPEN

Evolution, 76

MORTON BRYAN WHARTON, D.D.

The Denominational Team, 77

Folk Songs

ARKANSAS TRAVELER, *83*

THE BOLL WEEVIL SONG, *85*

CLAUDE ALLEN, *88*

THE DYING COWBOY, *90*

JESSE JAMES WAS HIS NAME, *94*

ROSA LECARSON

Little Mary Phagan, 96

THE KNOXVILLE GIRL, *98*

TOM DOOLEY, *100*

WILDWOOD FLOWER, *103*

THE WRECK ON THE C. & O., *104*

Home

(William) Hervey Allen

La Fayette Lands, 109

Carolina Spring Song, 115

John Henry Boner

The Wanderer Back Home, 117

George Graham Currie

Florida My Home, 119

(Edwin) DuBose Heyward

Dusk, 121

Modern Philosopher, 123

Judd Mortimer Lewis

Longing For Texas (1903), 124

John Charles McNeill

Away Down Home, 125

Jesse Covington, 127

"97": The Fast Mail, 128

Leonora Montero Martin

The Old North State: A Toast, 131

Turner Mouring

Song of the Arkansas, 132

George C. Stockard

Arkansas, 134

War Eagle, 137

About the Editor, 139

*The task of the civilized intelligence is one
of perpetual salvage. —Allen Tate*

FOREWORD

Our collection of Southern poets and poems, *The Land They Loved,* as stated in previous volumes, is made not from the viewpoint of a literary critic but from that of a historian interested in how the Southern people expressed their life and spirit in verse, a type of communication that carries its own kind of truth.

The New South, for historians, is the period from the end of Reconstruction to World War I. We have expanded the time period a bit at both ends.

The New South has not fared well in cultural commentary. Shortly after the end of this period, famously provocative H.L. Mencken portrayed the South as a "Desert of the Bozart," a backwater showing no presence of modern civilised culture, the *beaux* arts.

True the South was short on publishers, art museums, symphony orchestras, professional theatre, and the kind of "realist" writers that Mencken preferred, some of them now forgotten. The North had many wealthy men ready to invest in cultural prestige, the South few.

Mencken exaggerated and he was a very bad prophet. Writers like Grace King, Thomas Nelson Page, and Elizabeth Madox Roberts and others not contemptible were flourishing and widely read. Faulkner was soon to have the world marvel at his little postage stamp of territory in Mississippi. The Agrarians were beginning to gather at Vanderbilt, partly energised by Mencken's urban contempt for the Southern plain folk in his coverage of the Dayton Monkey Trial. The Charleston Poetry Society was fostering some pretty good writers.

Our poets' subjects are largely traditional: love of family, home, State, and the South; Christian faith; nature; life on the land; and romance. Further, they must deal, most of the time as positively as possible, with a society thrown into a bleak and impoverished state.

The two volumes of *Poets and Poems of the New South*, I am inclined to think, show an intellectual and artistic life with more than a little merit. Especially for a defeated and impoverished people. They certainly show some admirable minds and accomplished poets.

Clyde Wilson

Dutch Fork, South Carolina

Memory

Soldiers march! We shall not fight again
The Yankees with our guns well-aimed and rammed—
All are born Yankees of the race of men
And this, too, now the country of the damned
—Allen Tate, To the Lacedaemonians

J.E. BATAILE

Dedication of the Monument
to the Defenders of Vicksburg

Shades of our heroes dead,

Sleeping in glory,

Here, where your blood was shea,

Carve we your story!

Marble must sink in dust,

Fame lives forever.

Though your true blades be rust,

Forget we? Never!

Yon sculptured sentinel

Watches your sleeping.

Tells how you fought and fell,

Loyally keeping

Life's trust. You met death's hour

Stern and undaunted.

Ours 'tis to nurse the flower

Your valour planted.

Here,'neath the giant hills,

Rest warriors, rest ye!

Lulled by the murm'ring rills,

None shall molest ye!

Here,'neath the giant hills,

Rest warriors, rest ye!

Lulled by the murm'ring rills,

None shall molest ye!

Fanned by our south wind's breath,
Sleep, soldiers weary!
Yours was no fameless death,
Darksome and dreary.
Sleep well! The strife is past;
No war-drum's rattle
Breaks forth, nor bugle's blast.
Hushed is the battle.
Wrapt in your native earth,
Sweet be your slumber!
When shall we match your worth?
When your deeds number?
Strewn be this sacred sod,
Soldier's fit pillow.
Whence your souls sprang to God,
With sorrow's willow!
Many a youth shall bring
Many a maiden,
Tribute of balmy spring
Here, flower-laden.
Sleep on; but not for aye!
Should war's red chalice
Dash out its gory spray
Over our valleys,
Come! In the battle's crest
Flash your proud lances,
Lead where our bravest, best
Column advances!

♦ ♦ ♦

VIRGINIA FRAZER BOYLE (1863-1898) of Tennessee was a versatile poet and story writer, particularly known for her black characters like "Uncle Wash." A prodigy, at 14 she won a poetry prize from *Harper's Magazine* and was already unofficially preparing cases in her father's law office.

The Wizard of the Saddle

'Twas out of the South that the lion heart came,
From the ranks of the Gray like the flashing of flame,
A juggler with fortune, a master with fame—
The rugged heart born to command.

As he rode by the stars of an unconquered will,
And he struck with the might of an undaunted skill;
Unschooled, but as firm as the granite-flanked hill—
As true and as tried as steel.

Though the Grey were outnumbered, he counted no odd,
But fought like a demon and struck like a god,
Disclaiming defeat on the blood-curdled sod,
As he pledged to the South that he loved.

'Twas saddle and spur, or on foot in the field,
Unguided by tactics that knew how to yield;
Stripped of all, save his honour, but rich in that shield,
Full armoured by Nature's own hand.

As the rush of the storm, he swept on the foe;
It was "Come!" to his legions, he never said "Go!"
And with sinews unbending, how could the world know
That he rallied a starving host?

And the wondering ranks of the foe were like clay
To these men of flint in the molten day;
And the hell-hounds of war howled afar for their prey,
When the arm of a Forrest led.

For devil or angel, life stirred when he spoke,
And the current of courage, if slumbering, woke
At the yell of the leader, for never was broke,
The record, men wondering read

With a hundred he charged like a thousand men,
And the hoof-beats of one seemed the tattoo of ten;
What bar were burned bridges or flooded fords, when
The wizard of battles was there?

But his pity could bend to a fallen foe,
The mailed hand soothe a brother's woe;
There was time to be human, for tears to flow—
For the heart of the man to thrill.

Then "On!" as though never a halt befell,
With a swinging blade and the Rebel yell,
Through the song of the bullets and plowshares of hell—
The hero, half iron, half soul!

Swing, rustless blade in the dauntless hand;
Ride, soul of a god, through the deathless band,
Through the low green mounds or the breadth of the
land, Wherever your legions dwell!

Swing, Rebel blade, through the halls of fame,
Where courage and justice have left your name;
By the torches of glory your deeds shall flame
With the reckoning of Time!

◆ ◆ ◆

JOSIE FRAZEE CAPPLEMAN (1861-1936) of Arkansas published *Heart Songs* and was an active pioneer in the American Women' Club Movement.

The Old Time Darky

They are going fast, they're going
From the old-time cabin door,
And the places now that know them,
Will know them soon no more;
Aye, the "Uncle" and the "Aunty"
With the bygones soon will be,
And no more of "Mars" and "Missus"
Will there come to you and me.

No more the crooning "Mammy,"
Softly swaying to and fro;
With her love, unchanged, enduring,
Will the Southland's wee ones know.
No more that careless sing-song,
In measure quaint and droll,
Will o'erflow from hearts so happy
Till of music seemed each soul.

No more that admiration
And that darky-pride, so great,
In all the fleecy acres
Of his master's vast estate;
No more that fond affection
For the household on the hill;
For the trusty, old-time darky
Had no equal and ne'er will.

No more that joy, the wildest
That a rustic race e'er knew,
When the Christmas feasts were ready
And that day no work to do;
Or, the marriage of "Young Missus"
To some magnate of the land,
When the darky shared the glory
Of the bravest of that band.

No more that grief profoundest,
When "Old Mars" or "Missus" died,
Or the baby from the "big house,"
Was lowered by their side;
For the darky mourned as truly
For the Master and his kind,
As the faithful in the annals
Of grief, we ever find.

And to me one old "Black, Aunty"
Still is spared tho' brief her days,
And I oft in silence wonder
At her dear old darky ways;
Still, when sickness comes, or sorrow,
Other friends may faint and fall,
But "Black Mammy" never falters-
She is faithful through it all.

With a heart surcharged with sorrow,
Do I watch them pass away,
For the Old South with them endeth
And the New assumes its sway—
With the passing of the darky
Of that good, old, golden time,
So passeth out forever
That fair epoch of our clime.

♦ ♦ ♦

EDWARD WARD CARMACK (1858-1908) was a newspaper-man and U.S. Representative and Senator from Tennessee 1897-1907.Carmack's statue stood before the Tennessee state capitol for many years, but was destroyed in an ethnic cleansing riot in 2020.

The South...

The SOUTH is a land that has known sorrows! it is a land that has broken the ashen crust and moistened it with tears; a land scarred and riven by the ploughshare of war and billowed with the graves of her dead; but a land of legend, a land of song, a land of hallowed and heroic memories.

To that land every drop of my blood, every fiber of my being, every pulsation of my heart, is consecrated forever. I was born of her womb; I was nurtured at her breast; and when my last hour shall come, I pray GOD that I may be pillowed upon her bosom and rocked to sleep within her tender and encircling arms.

◆ ◆ ◆

WILLIAM LAWRENCE CHITENDEN (1862-1934) was born and raised in New Jersey. In 1887, he came to Texas to manage a cattle ranch and was thereafter an inspired poet of the Lone Star Republic.

"Remember The Alamo"

Fair Greece and Rome brave heroes knew,

But Texas has her heroes, too,

The men of Alamo!

That bold, courageous, noble band

Of rangers in the border land,

Who fighting fell with sword in hand,

At San Antonio!

Their well-remembered woes and wrongs

Demand no feeble minstrel's songs,

For history's fame is theirs.

Their names shall live on mortal tongue,

Their deeds of valor long be sung,

Their memories blessed by old and young

In silent tears and prayers.

Dark Gettysburg and Waterloo

Survivors from their carnage knew,

Thermopylae had one!

But on the Lone Star's gory field

The Texans bled, but would not yield;

Each man died fighting on his shield-
The Alamo left none!
Crockett, Travis, and Bowie's names
Shall glow with Freedom's holy flames
And brighten Glory's sheath!
No lettered urn or flowered perfume
Need mark such storied heroes' tomb,
For honors round their names shall bloom
In an immortal wreath!

♦

My Old Friend, "The Majah Green"

In the sunny land of Texas, where Tom Ochiltree's at home,
Where the cowman swings the lasso and the wild
    jack-rabbits roam;
Where hearts of gallant gentlemen are full of sand and glow,
And the prairies laugh to plenty with the tickle of the hoe;
Where the vote is always solid-on the Democratic side,
And old "Tariff Mills" is grinding grist and thought from
    far and wide;
Where the mocking birds are singing on the feathery
    mesquite trees,
And the zephyrs soft are flinging rarest fragrance to the breeze;
Where the rustlers from the ranches chase the wild-eyed
    maverick steer,
And the pitching pony prances o'er the dog-towns far and near;
Where the antelope is grazing, thirty miles from Abilene,
There it was I met the "Majah"— my old friend, "The Majah Green."

He had led the Southern armies, when their banners floated free,
From the winding Rappahannock to the tropic Mexique Sea.
Ay, he told me wondrous stories of the days "befo' de wah,"
When he "owned the pertest darkies," "that was raised in
    Georgah, sah."
And he spoke about his boyhood in a "rah old Southern town,"
On the lazy Ocamulgee, with its houses old and brown;
Where they raised big sweet potatoes, and the "little goober vines,"
And the "roses blushed forever," 'neath the softly wooing pines.

But at last he came to Texas, to the "woolly wild" frontier,
Where he "founded Anson City," in the springtime of the year.
But at last he came to Texas, to the "woolly wild" frontier,
Where he "founded Anson City," in the springtime of the year.
There he built his "little homestead," garlanded with eglantine,
Where the hollyhocks threw kisses to the fragrant jessamine.
He was bluff and stout and hearty, rather pompous in his mien,
Yet he had a kindly "howdy" for all, had Major Green.

Perhaps he was not educated, as a tenderfoot conceives,
But he scanned the books of Nature, as the seasons turned
      the leaves.
He was very fond of hunting that's the reason he liked me;
Many a time we roamed together o'er the prairies broad and free,
Where the Double Mountain standeth, and will stand for many a day,
Till the Seventh Trumpet soundeth, and the earth shall pass away.
Oft we watched the gilded banners of the golden hours depart,
When the twilight's richest beauty sheds its shadows o'er the heart.
Oft we watched the gilded banners of the golden hours depart,
When the twilight's richest beauty sheds its shadows o'er the heart.
Soon the evening fire was kindled, and we rested on the ground,
While the breathing stars shed lustre o'er the wilderness profound.
Then the Major told his stories, sang some deep bass roundelay
To his "Lily of the Valley" or "Old Dixie," far away.
Yes, his heart beat high but kindly, square and honest, nothing mean
'Bout that "Vetran, sah," "the Majah," my old friend, the Major Green.

Hark! the lonely doves are cooing, in the weeping mesquite vale,
And the south winds sad are sighing o'er the old McKenzie trail;
Ah, they miss that sturdy figure, for his honest feet have trod
Far beyond the sunset mountains where his spirit went to God.
The prairie flowers are waving o'er a lonely little mound,
For the Major roams the borders of the Happy Hunting Ground.
The prairie flowers are waving o'er a lonely little mound,
For the Major roams the borders of the Happy Hunting Ground.
He has crossed the Royal River that rolls on to crystal seas,
And has found his old commander, Stonewall Jackson,
        "neath the trees."
They are resting from their labors; oh, I know that smile serene
That in olden days illumined my old friend, "The Majah Green."

◆

Old Fort Phantom Hill

(An abandoned fort in Jones County, Texas. Supposed to be haunted.)

On the breezy Texas border, on the prairies far away,
Where the antelope is grazing and the Spanish ponies play;
Where the tawny cattle wander through the golden incensed hours,
And the sunlight woos a landscape clothed in royal robes of flowers;
Where the Elm and Clear Fork mingle, as they journey to the sea,
And the night-wind sobs sad stories o'er a wild and lonely lea;
Where of old the dusky savage and the shaggy bison trod,
And the reverent plains are sleeping 'midst drowsy dreams of God;
Where the twilight loves to linger, e'er night's sable robes are cast
'Round grim-ruined, spectral chimneys, telling stories of the past,
There upon an airy mesa, close beside a whispering rill,
There to-day you'll find the ruins of the Old Fort Phantom Hill.

Years ago, so runs the legend, 'bout the year of Fifty-three,
This old fort was first established by the gallant soldier, Lee;
And to-day the restless spirits of his proud and martial band
Haunt those ghostly, gloomy chimneys in the Texas border-land.
There once every year at midnight, when the chilling Northers roar,
And the storm-king breathes its thunder from the heights of Labrador,
When the vaulted gloom re-echoes with the owls- "whit-tu-woo!"
And the stealthy cayote answers with his lonely, long "ki-oo!"
And the stealthy cayote answers with his lonely, long "ki-oo!"
Then strange phantoms flit in silence through that weeping
    mesquite vale,

And the reveilles come sounding o'er the old McKenzie Trail,
Then the muffled drums beat muster and the bugles sadly trill,
And the vanished soldiers gather round the heights of
     Phantom Hill.

Then pale bivouac fires are lighted and those gloomy chimneys glow,
While the grizzled veterans muster from the taps of long ago,
Lee and Johnston and McKenzie, Grant and Jackson,
     Custer, too,
Gather there in peaceful silence waiting for their last review;
Blue and gray at length united on the high redoubts of fame,
Soldiers all in one grand army, that will answer in God's name.
Yes, they rest on heights of glory in that fair, celestial world,
"Where the war-drum throbs no longer, and the battle-flags
     are furled."
Yes, they rest on heights of glory in that fair, celestial world,
"Where the war-drum throbs no longer, and the battle-flags
     are furled."
And to-day the birds are singing where was heard the cannons' roar,
For the gentle doves are nesting 'midst those ruins of the war.
Yes, the mocking-birds re-echo: "Peace on earth, to men good will,"
And the "swords are turned to ploughshares" in the land of
     Phantom Hill.

♦ ♦ ♦

COLUMBUS DREW (1820-1891) of Florida was a journalist and public official and a prolific poet of the second half of the 19th century—celebrating the Confederacy and his adopted State of Florida. His work appears in the two volumes of *The Land They Loved* preceding this.

Dedication of the Soldiers' Monument Tallahassee. 1880

We rear the monumental pile

To heroes that have passed away,

Like those in classic times, the while

Pure in our eyes as they

None left to time a prouder story,

None wear upon their martial brow

A halo crown of brighter glory

Than those we honour now

As flames from holy altars rise,

Remembrance from the patriot's breast

Will shine as fire that never dies,

To light the silent sleeper's rest;

And as a beacon to our gaze,

Though storms' round life be sweeping,

Upon this shaft in light shall blaze:

"He hath Them in His keeping"

"Firm as a Rock God's truth shall stand,"
Firm as our love this shaft shall keep
The memory of our Patriot band
Our noblest, best, that sleep.
If grander cenotaphs display
Proud deeds, or loftier towers,
Neither prouder deeds nor grander day
They consecrate than ours

Fair name, our Florida! Fair name,
Our land! Some, our brave, here sleep,
'Tis not the trump of empty fame
We sound above your graves We weep,
And hear the plaintive tear-drops fall,
Like pass-words near the grassy tent,
That to the waiting slumberers call
From out the starry firmament.

♦

The Prayer of Milo Cooper

(Drew wrote this last poem in 1891 on reports of the trip of the former slave Milo Cooper from Orlando, Florida, to New Orleans to visit his dying former master Jefferson Davis.)

There was whispering in the chamber, there was soundless tread of feet

As though the whispers and the tread of soundless steps were meet;

The couch the loving watch bent o'er, with tearful, hopeful eyes,

Was still, as one who resting there breathes a last breath and dies;

For death had filled its mission, and the sleeper heard the call.

It came to him a whisper, death entering the door;

Only a peaceful whisper of the simple words, "No more!"

There hurried to the bedside one who traveled far to see

The sick one; faithful visitor! as faithful as could be.

In times gone by they called him *slave*, his heart was as before

Bound to his master; freedman now and called a slave no more.

His hair was white, and Time had seemed to trace his brow more deep

Than when he served. He heard the woe, and came to serve and weep.

A broken tie had made him free of limb to come and go,

The tie of love he kept unbroke, his heart had willed it so.

Even the whispering of the room grew still when the old face

Looked in, permitted gladly near the dead to have a place.

He entered; soon upon his knees beside the bed he prayed
A prayer of blessing for the dead, the grandest ever made—
A prayer that gathered in a look the deeds of good for years
The slave and master did for each, now jeweled in his tears.
Oh, mightiest prayer of him who spoke, the slave who humbly knelt
Beside the master when the bonds of slave were never felt!
But only bonds of loyalty to every trait of good
A noble being cherished, and as nobly understood.
The black and white were types of things well written for the guide
Of lives by golden rule decreed until the master died.

There were whisperings in the chamber, there are whisperings in
    the breast,
Of the prayer old Milo Cooper prayed beside the dead at rest.
He came self-bonded freeman, the closing eye to see;
He found a glory on the face: the master too was free!

◆ ◆ ◆

PAUL LAURENCE DUNBAR (1872-1906) was born in Ohio to parents who had been slaves in Kentucky. Although he was tubercular and died at 33 he left a large body of poetry and fiction. Dunbar is certainly the most important African American writer of the 19th century if not of all time. His verse covers a large range of subjects in both dialect and literary English. It will be seen that his views as an African American did not always coincide with what is usually assumed they should be.

Chrismus On the Plantation

It was Chrismus Eve, I mind hit fu' a mighty gloomy day —

Bofe de weathah an' de people-not a one of us was gay:

Cose you'll t'ink dat's mighty funny 'twell I try to mek hit cleah,

Fu' a da'ky's allus happy when de holidays is neah.

But we wasn't, fu' dat mo'nin' Mastah 'd tol' us we mus' go,

He'd been payin' us sence freedom, but he couldn't pay no mo':

He wa'n't nevah used to plannin' 'fo' he got so po' an' ol'

So he gwine to give up tryin', an' de homestead mus' be sol'.

1 kin see him stan'in' now erpon de step ez cleah ez day,

Wid de win' a-kind o' fondlin' thoo his haih all thin an' gray;

An' I'membah how he trimbled when he said, "It's ha'd fu' me,

Not to mek yo' Chrismus brightah, but I 'low it wa'n't to be."

All de women was a-cryin', an' de men, too, on de sly,

An' I noticed somep'n shinin' even in ol' Mastah's eye.

But we all stood still to listen ez ol' Ben come f'om de crowd

An' spoke up, a-try'n' to steady down his voice and mek it loud:—

"Look hyeah, Mastah, I's been servin' you' fu' lo! dese many yeahs,
An' now, sence we's got freedom an' you's kind o' po', hit 'pears
Dat you want us all to leave you 'cause you don't t'ink you can pay.
Ef my membry has n't fooled me, seem dat whut I hyead you say.

Er in othah wo'ds, you wants us to fu'git dat you's been kin',
An' ez soon ez you is he'pless, we's to leave you hyeah behin.
Well, ef dat's de way dis freedom ac's on people, white er black,
You kin jes' tell Mistah Lincum fu' to tek his freedom back.

"We gwine wo'k dis ol' plantation fu' whatevah we kin git,
Fu' I know hit did suppo't us, an' de place kin do it yit.
Now de land is yo's, de hands is ouahs, an' I reckon we 'll be brave,
An' we'll bah ez much ez you do w'en we has to scrape an' save."

Ol' Mastah stood dah trimblin', but a-smilin' thoo his teahs,
An' den hit seemed jes' nachul-like, de place fah rung wid cheahs,
An' soon ez dey was quiet, some one sta'ted sof an' low:
"Praise God," an' den we all jined in, "from whom all blessin's flow!"

Well, dey was n't no use tryin', ouah min's was sot to stay,
An' po' ol' Mastah could n't plead ner baig, ner drive us way,
An' all at once, hit seemed to us, de day was bright agin, So
evahone was gay dat night, an' watched de Chrismus in.

♦

After A Visit

I be'n down in ole Kentucky
    Fur a week er two, an' say,
"T wuz ez hard ez breakin' oxen
    Fur to tear myse'f away.
Allus argerin' 'bout fren'ship
    An' yer hospitality—
Y' ain't no right to talk about it
    Tell you be'n down there to see.

See jest how they give you welcome
    To the best that's in the land,
Feel the sort o' grip they give you
    When they take you by the hand.
Hear 'em say, "We're glad to have you,
    Better stay a week er two;"
An' the way they treat you makes you
    Feel that ev'ry word is true.

Feed you tell you hear the buttons
    Crackin' on yore Sunday vest;
Haul you roun' to see the wonders
    Tell you have to cry for rest.
Drink yer health an' pet an' praise you
    Tell you git to feel ez great
Ez the Sheriff o' the county
    Er the Gov'ner o' the State.

Wife, she sez I must be crazy
    'Cause I go on so, an' Nelse
He 'lows, "Goodness gracious! daddy,
    Cain't you talk about nuthin' else?"
Well, pleg-gone it, I'm jes' tickled,
    Bein' tickled ain't no sin;
I be'n down in ole Kentucky,
    An' I want o' go ag'in

◆ ◆ ◆

ARMISTEAD CHURCHILL GORDON (1855-1931) of Virginia was a lawyer and for many years Rector of the University of Virginia. He was a prolific poet and the author of 15 works of history. His verse also appears in vol. 3 of *The Land They Loved*.

The Little Old Church

I went to the little church to-day
Over the brook, beyond the hill.
It looks as it looked when I went away,
Green-yarded and white-paled still.

I was a youth when I crossed the sea
To wander in foreign lands, and lo!
Now there is gray in my beard. Ah, me!
Can it be so long ago?

There used to be in those far-back years
A little girl with a happy face,
And a sweet, strange fashion of smiles and tears,
And a young fawn's agile grace,

Who sat each Sunday serenely there
In that little church, where the sunlight fell
Through the window over her yellow hair
And over her face ah, well!

Ah, well! And I—oh, that little maid,
I loved her truly. Each Sabbath day
I'd go there and watch how the sunshine played
In her hair, ere I went away.

Ere I went away. That was long years back,
And now I am middle-aged, forsooth.
It is hard that a brave, strong lad, good lack,
Must give up his brave, strong youth,

While a little church for years can seem
Unchanged. Why, to-day they sang that strain
That they sang long ago it was like a dream
Of my dead youth come again.

I sat in a dim, back-corner pew
Where I sat when a boy, and closed my eyes,
Till thoughts of the past and the present grew
Into solemn mysteries.

I dreamed I was young again-that there
In the seat three paces in front of me
The sunshine was dancing on yellow hair,
And I thought: "Can this thing be?

"I went to her grave 'neath the churchyard tree
On this very morn, ere I came in here,
Where I thought of the things that used to be
Till I felt on my face a tear.

"And now to think if I open my eyes
I shall see her kneel in that pew and pray
With a soul that is ready for Paradise
As I did ere I went away!"

I opened my eyes and looked, but lo!
The pew was empty. The sunlight strayed
Up and down on the cushioned seat, as though
It sought for the little maid.

A butterfly drifted in, and flew
For a moment about, then out again.
"Into my life she came, like you
And went," I faltered in pain.

And the pastor read, "Even as water spilled
On the ground, that cannot be gathered again,
Are the children of men," and the sad words filled
My soul with a sadder pain.

When lo! the butterfly drifted in
Once more, and the pastor's lips then read,
"As little children are, free from sin."
"She is gathered to God," I said.

And I said, "You went, but you have returned,
I shall see her again in the years to be—
In the years to be!" And my cold heart burned
By the wayside there in me.

I had not entered for many years
A church of Christ, as I did to-day.
Till this morning mine eyes had not known tears
Since the time when I went away.

I think I shall go to this church always,
Till they carry me out to the graveyard tree,
For the sake of that dear girl's sweet young face,
And the days that used to be.

♦ ♦ ♦

CLIFFORD ANDERSON LANIER (1844-1908) of Alabama was the younger brother of Sidney Lanier. At 16 Clifford insisted on joining the Confederate army with his brother. While they were serving on a blockade runner Sidney was captured although Clifford made a daring escape. After the war, Clifford Lanier was a businessman in Montgomery, Alabama, and published novels and poetry.

The First Confederate White House

Memento-hallowed of heroic Lost,

Nor time, nor rust hath power to despoil,

Nor hate besmirch thee with deflow ring moil!

The pain of martyrs made thy priceless cost,

With outpoured blood of brave Confederate host,

And free-will offerings pure of corn and oil;

Thus thou art worthy countless lovers' toil;

Who suffered all for love now love thee most.

Reborn, rechristened, and by love new-made,

Thou art the dearer for what ruin wrought;

Reborn, rechristened, and by love new-made,

Thou art the dearer for what ruin wrought;

With thee let treasured memories be laid

For keeping, as to shrines our dead are brought;

Let Truth of history gem thy casket gold,

And thou stay ever new, yet ever old.

♦ ♦ ♦

CARLYLE McKINLEY (1847-1904) of South Carolina left the University of Georgia at the age of 15 to join the Confederate army. After the war he became a prominent staff member of the *Charleston News & Courier*. He wrote the first books about the Charleston hurricane of 1885 and earthquake of 1886. His verse also appears in volume 3 of *The Land They Loved*. A small granite marker was later placed at Timrod's grave at Trinity Episcopal Church, Columbia, SC.

At Timrod's Grave

Harp of the South! no more, no more
Thy silvery strings shall quiver,
The one strong hand might win thy strains
Is chilled and stilled forever.

Our one sweet singer breaks no more
The silence sad and long,
The land is hushed from shore to shore,
It brooks no feebler song!

No other voice can charm our ears,
None other soothe our pain;
Better these echoes lingering yet
Than any ruder strain.

For singing, Fate hath given sighs,
For music we make moan;
Ah! who may touch the harp strings since
That whisper—"He is gone!"

See where he lies— his last sad home
Of all memorial bare,
Save for a little heap of leaves
The winds have gathered there!

One fair, frail shell from some far sea
Lies lone above his breast,
Sad emblem and sole epitaph
To mark his place of rest.

The sweet winds murmur in its heart
A music soft and low,
As they would bring their secrets still
To him who sleeps below.

And lo! one tender pearly bloom,
Through weeds and leave upcast;
As some sweet thought he left unsung
Were blossoming at last.

Wild weeds grow rank about the place,
A dark, cold spot, and drear;
The dull neglect that marked his life
Hath followed even here.

Around shine many a marble shaft
And polished pillar fair,
And strangers stand at Timrod's grave
To praise them unaware!

"Hold up the glories of thy dead!"
To thine own self be true,
Land that he loved! Come, honor now
This grave that honors you!

♦ ♦ ♦

JOHN TROTWOOD MOORE (1858-1929) of Tennessee was a prolific author of poetry, fiction, and history. From 1919-1929 he was the State Librarian of Tennessee. He was the father of well-known 20th century poet Merrill Moore. In the 1880s, he made a speech dedicating a plaque to Jefferson Davis at an Episcopal Church in Montgomery, Alabama. The plaque was removed in the cultural cleansing of 2019.

Sam Davis

"Tell me his name and you are free,"
The General said, while from the tree
The grim rope dangled threat' ningly.

The birds ceased singing—happy birds,
That sang of home and mother-words,
The sunshine kissed his cheek—dear sun;
It loves a life that's just begun!
The very breezes held their breath
To watch the fight twixt life and death.
The very breezes held their breath
To watch the fight twixt life and death.
And O, how calm and sweet and free,
Smiled back the hills of Tennessee!
Smiled back the hills, as if to say,
"O, save your life for us to-day."

"Tell me his name and you are free,"
The General said, "and I shall see
You safe within the rebel line—
I'd love to save such life as thine."

A tear gleamed down the ranks of blue—
(The bayonets were tipped with dew),
Across the rugged cheek of war
God's angels rolled a teary star.
The boy looked up— twas this they heard:
"And would you have me break my word?"

A tear stood in the General's eye!
"My boy, I hate to see thee die—
Give me the traitor's name and fly!"

Young Davis smiled, as calm and free
As He who walked on Galilee:
"Had I a thousand lives to live,
Had I a thousand lives to give,
I'd lose them, nay, I'd gladly die
Before I'd live one life, a lie!"
He turned —for not a soldier stirred—
"Your duty, men—I gave my word."

The hills smiled back a farewell smile,
The breeze sobbed o'er his hair awhile,
The birds broke out in sad refrain,
The sunbeams kissed his cheek again—
Then, gathering up their blazing bars,
They shook his name among the stars.

O Stars, that now his brothers are,
    O Sun, his sire in truth and light,
Go tell the list'ning worlds afar
    Of him who died for truth and right!
For martyr of all martyrs he
Who dies to save an enemy!

◆ ◆ ◆

CLARENCE N. OUSLEY (1863-1948) was a popular journalist and public official and the author of several books of history.

When the Mint is in the Liquor

When the mint is in the liquor and its fragrance on the glass
It breathes a recollection that can never, never pass
When the South was in the glory of a never-ending June,
The strings were on the banjo and the fiddle was in tune,
And we reveled in the plenty that we thought could never pass
And lingered at the julep in the ever-brimming glass.

There was mettle in the morning and adventure in the chase
And Beauty sat the saddle with the poetry of grace;
And the singing of the darkies in the cotton and the corn
Was chorused with the echo of the old familiar horn.
There was splendor in the glamour of the canopy at noon,
And sweetness in the languor of the lazy afternoon,
And the breezes of the evening were the breathings of romance
That quickened into whispers in the rapture of the dance,
While the banjo in the cabin and the fiddle in the hall
With music filled the measure of the night's ecstatic thrall.

O, the beauty of the Southland in the splendor of its prime,
The fragrance and the plenty of a radiant summer time,
When we reveled in the glory that we thought could never pass,
And lingered at the julep in the ever-brimming glass.

◆ ◆ ◆

THOMAS NELSON PAGE (1853-1922) of Virginia, though not known as a poet, was perhaps the most important and successful Southern writer of the post-Reconstruction period. Page was a friend of Theodore Roosevelt and Woodrow Wilson and was the U.S. Minister to Italy during the World War I era. His stories of old Virginia were immensely popular with Northern readers and were important in alleviating Northern hostility. This brief selection gives an idea of his most popular novels and stories.

Uncle Gabe's White Folks

"Fine ole place?" Yes, suh, 't is so;

An' mighty fine people my white folks war

But you ought ter 'a' seen it years ago,

When de Marster an' de Mistis lived up dyah:

When de niggers'd stan' all roun' de do,

Like grains o' corn on de cornhouse flo.

"Live' mons'ous high?" Yes, Marster, yes;

D' cut 'n' onroyal 'n' gordly dash;

Eat an' drink till you could n' res'.

My folks war n' none o' yo' po'-white-trash;

Nor, suh, dey was of high degree

Dis heah nigger am quality!

♦ ♦ ♦

CALE YOUNG RICE (1872-1943) of Kentucky was best known as a playwright. His wife was the novelist Alice Hegan Rice whose *Mrs. Wiggs of the Cabbage Patch* was translated into European languages and four times made into a movie.

Daniel Boone's Last Look Westward

I'm only four score year, my sons, and a few

To fill the measure up. And so I shouldn't

Be shut here like an old hound by the fire

To dream of deeds I still have wind to do.

Maybe I have performed enough for one man;

For there's Kentucky cut from the wilderness

And sewed fast to the States by law and order—

Which I'm not sayin' isn't good for them

Who like pullin' in harness with their neighbors.

But I keep seein' trails,— runnin' to westward

And northwest, Indian-footed trails

That no white man has ever pierced an eye through;

And beyond them are prairie lands and forests

Which settlers comin' after me could scalp

And sell, if silver is the game they're seekin':

And the Almighty means my eyes to see them,

Else He'd have made my sight dim and rheumy

By now-and where's the deer or bear that gambols

Before my gun and goes away to say so?

It's kind of shiftless maybe, I'll allow,
To want to keep always beyond the settlements
Not in them: ten near families is too many.
But the Lord never meant the plow to be
My instrument: I get to the end of a furrow
And there's the wilderness waitin', all creation,
And I just have to find a path across it—
As your ma, there, knows; though I never could tell her
The reason, till they took Kentucky in.
And then I saw the cunnin' to be wise
With animals and savages was more
Than love of powder and shot; and that God used
My axe to hew a realm out. And there's more realms
Yet to be hewed and God's grindin' the axes,
I'll tell you that. For, young Lewis and Clark,
Sons of my two old friends, are comin' tomorrow
With unblazed trails of the Northwest in their eyes;
And who knows but that land's as big as Kentucky
And Illinois too; and that they're comin'
For more than to look at an old hound by the fire?
There's one run in me yet; and if I died
Somewhere upon a far new trail with them,
There's a coffin-board saved-and I'd sleep better ...

Unless your ma, this time, wouldn't be a willin'
To pack my kit and draw the latch of the door.
She won't, eh? Then it's dodderin' here, I reckon,
And dreamin'. Put a fresh log on, and let be.
Young Lewis and Clark will need a-many like me, though,
Before they hew that Northwest into the world.

◆ ◆ ◆

GILBERT MOXLEY SORRELL (1838-1901) of Georgia served throughout the War between the States on the staff of General Longstreet. He left this tribute to Lee in his memoir, *Recollections of a Confederate Staff Officer*, published in 1905.

(From his memoirs, on Lee)

Ah Muse! You dare not claim
A nobler man than he,
Nor nobler man has less of blame
Nor blameless man has purer name,
Nor purer man hath grander fame,
Nor fame, another Lee!

♦ ♦ ♦

ZULA CAMILLE VAUGHAN of Arkansas.

"Dixie"

No other strain my soul can fill
Or start the tears so soon,
My being's deepest pulses thrill
Like the sweet Southern tune;
So sadly sweet, I'll ne'er decide
Whether pleasure 'tis or pain
Ne'er bugle breathed, or cornet sighed
A more impassioned strain.

O, can'st thou hear, and tamely stand,
Dost not the hot blood stir?
'T would nerve e'en cowards feeble brand
Strong as Excalibur!
It sounds-we hear the cannon roar,
Swift swords from scabbards fly,
We lead the gallant charge; once more,
Our Southern flag streams high.

O, martial air that nerved our dead
It seems to say to me
Those stirring strains your fathers led
To death, or victory,
And when they rose above the shriek
Of battle fierce and wild
They fired the strong, they nerved the weak
The dying heard and smiled.

Not France's glorious Marseillaise
Not Watch Song on the Rhine,
Nor homesick Switzer's Alpine lays
Touch such deep chords as thine.
Say, Veteran, who wore the grey,
And thrilled beneath that strain,
Leaps not your heart the same old way
When "Dixie's" played again?

◆ ◆ ◆

(MARIA) HOWARD WEEDEN (1846-1905) of Alabama was best known as a painter. She was well educated in art and literature. As a teenager, with her mother and sisters, she was driven out of her home in Huntsville by the Yankee occupiers. On a postwar visit to a Chicago exhibition Weeden was offended by the demeaning caricatures with which freed African Americans were portrayed. From *The Encyclopedia of Alabama*: "Maria Howard Weeden believed that the common portrayal of the freed people in her day lacked individuality and character. Her goal became to record the images of the free people whom she knew with love and respect and also to record the stories she heard them tell for future generations." She painted a remarkable gallery of portraits of Southern black people and published four books of poetry with her own illustrations.

The Banjo of the Past

YOU ax about dat music made
On banjos long ago,
An' wants to know why it ain't played
By niggers any mo'.

Dem banjos b'longed to by-gone days
When times an' chunes was rare,
When we was gay as children—'case
We didn't have a care.

But when we got our freedom, we
Found projeckin' was done;
Our livin' was to make—you see,
An' dat lef' out de fun.

We learned to vote an' read an' spell,
We learned de taste ob tears—
An' when you gets dat 'sponsible,
De banjo disappears!

♦

Beaten Biscuit

Of course I'll gladly give de rule
I meks beat-tiscuit by,
Dough I ain't sure dat you will mek
Dat bread de same as I.

'Case cooking's like religion is —
Some's 'lected, an' some ain't,
An' rules don't no more mek a cook,
Den sermons mek a Saint.

Well, 'bout de 'grediances required,
I needn't mention dem,
Of course you knows of flour an' things,
How much to put, an' whene.

But soon as you is got dat dough
Mixed up all smoove an' neat,
Den's when your genius gwine to show,
To get them biscuit beat!

Two hundred licks is what I gives
For home-folks, never fewer,
An' if I'm spectin' company in,
I gives five hundred sure!

♦

The Worst of War

When my young master went to war
He carried me wid him too,
An' dough I never fired a shot
Dere was plenty else to do.

He wore de sword an' buttons an' spurs,
But never so hard a thing did he do
As the thing he lef for me.

Where a storm of leaden hail fell thick
He got a ball in his heart
An' died wid a happy smile on his face—
But mine was de harder part:

I led his horse back home where dey sat
Expectin' him an' I saw
Mistis' an' Master's hearts when dey broke
An' dat was de worst of war!

♦

A Voice of the Night

Wide and warm lies the Southern night,
Steeped in purple dusk;
Calm except for the scented winds
That stir the jessamine's musk,
And silent—until a sudden Voice
Piercing the night is heard,
And the quiet, fragrant world awakes
To the song of a Mocking-bird.

Was it a dream that suddenly stirred
The sleeping bird to bliss
And woke his passionate eager heart
To rapture such as this?
Or was it that, from his lofty nest,
He saw in the East a ray
Of faint but certain dawn-and laughed
Because of Hope and Day!

♦

Mother and Mammy

Among the ranks of shining saints
Disguised in heavenly splendour,
Two Mother-faces wait for me,
Familiar still, and tender.

One face shines whiter than the dawn,
And steadfast as a star;
None but my Mother's face could shine
So bright—and be so far!

The other dark one leans from Heaven,
Brooding still to calm me;
Black as if ebon Rest had found
Its image in my Mammy!

◆

The Old Boatman

I changed my name when I got free,
To "Mister" like the res',
But now dat I am going Home,
I likes de ol' name bes'.

Sweet voices callin' "Uncle Rome,"
Seem ringin' in my ears;
An' swearin' sort o' sociable,
Ol' Master's voice I hears.

De way he used to call his boat,
Across de river: "Rome!
You damn ol' nigger, come an' bring
Dat boat, an' row me home!"

He's passed Heaven's River now, an' soon
He'll call across its foam:
"You, Rome, you damn ol' nigger, loose
Your boat, an' come on Home!"

♦

When Manners Were in Bloom

You say you would paint my manners too
Along wid my head—if you could;
Well, you should have lived in olden times
When manners was really good!

De days was sweet an' warm an' long,
Wid plenty of time to be kine,
An' every one smiled an' bowed an' scraped
An' every one did it fine!

I seem to smell de locust flower
Heavy after rain—
An' de ghostly scent of mimosa blooms
Comes blowin' back again;

An' I feels de fine ole mannerly times
Mix wid de scents till I seem
To see ole Master as natchel as life-
Bow in a kin' of dream:

His manners was certainly quality ways,
De finest dat ever I see;
Dough folks used to laugh an' say dat he took
Dem gilt-edged ways from me!

♦ ♦ ♦

FAITH

MARY BAYARD DEVEREUX CLARKE (1827- 1886) of North Carolina was a learned, versatile, and prolific poet and translator who was widely published in Europe and America. Her verse appears in volumes 2 and 3 of *The Land They Loved*.

John Wesley's Foot-Print

The summer sun was shining bright
On Epworth church one Sunday morn,
When grand John Wesley humbly came
Back, to the town where he was born.

Back to its little parish church
In singleness of heart he turned,
To preach that all should practice, what
Within its sacred walls he'd learned.

A gathering crowd his steps attend,
And soon the church's door they reach;
Alas! they found it shut and barred;
Within its walls he might not preach.

The crowd, indignant, murmured loud,
But Wesley only waved his hand;
And turning to his father's grave,
Upon the tomb-stone took his stand.

"The church, my friends, is dark and cold,
But warmed by God's own glorious sun,
I'll from this pulpit preach so plain,
That all may read e'en while they run."

'Twas nothing new he taught that day,
But ah! its mem'ry lingers yet,
And Epworth shows upon that stone,
The print where Wesley's foot was set.

'Tis but a legend, yet it folds,
Within its heart a lesson grand;
That summer sun, that close shut door,
The murmuring crowd that round it stand.

For Wesley taught God's tender love
Within no single church is barred,
And left his foot-print on the age,
If not upon that marble hard.

♦

(For I shall have to speak of the new faith in matter, once and still
so flouted and despised, now seen to be the haunt of mystery and
the home of thought." —Chadwick)

Matter

What is this matter over which

There rages theologic strife,

'Gainst him who says that it contains

"Promise and potency of life?"

Why is it scorned and flouted so?

Why counted gross and low?

If we believe apart from it,

The mind can no existence know.

If matter's indestructible,

Why is it such a deadly sin

To hold, that through eternity

As now, it evermore has been?

They're Truth's apostles, those who trace

Its grand illimitable past;

And read those laws which ne'er begun

And through eternity must last.

And they, whom some material call,

View matter with most solemn awe;

The womb of thought, of soul, of life,

The haunt of mystery and of law.

They may not know what law combines
Matter and mind, body and soul,
Nor how eternally it works,
Producing one harmonious whole.

'Tis but a part that they can see
Of that eternal living mind
Which dwells in nature, as the soul
And body are in one combined.

For how can one who's never known
The sense of smell conceive its power?
He cannot see, he cannot touch
The perfume rising from a flower.

Nor can the sense of man conceive
Matter etherealized-refined.
He cannot see, he cannot touch
His life, his soul, his conscious mind.

Then count me as a materialist
When matter's potency I plead;
And say it has eternal laws,
Man's finite senses cannot read.

◆

The Happy Valley

In the heart of Carolina, by the Blue Ridge girded round,
May the fabled Happy Valley of Rasselas be found;
By the rushing of the waters it was hollowed from the stone,
When the earth was hot and molten ere a single plant had grown;
And by the tramp of ages was slowly worn away,
Till the breath of life came stealing down the canon bare and gray,
Then Nature threw her mantle o'er the mountain's rugged side,
And smiled upon the valley, till with laughter it replied:
And she said, 'Till make a garden in the hollow of my hand,
With the water racing round it, like a sparkling jeweled band.
Here summer's heat I'll temper, and lighten winter's snow,
While from the earth forever shall healing waters flow."
Right royally the mother has kept her gracious word,
For the laughter of the waters in the vale is always heard;
While a 'broidery of flowers, the loveliest ever seen
Casts the colors of the rainbow o'er her robe of living green.
On the grass she threw her sceptre, and the golden-rod upsprung,
While a drapery of creepers o'er each precipice she hung;
Where in autumn like gay banners on battlements of old,
From her fortress they are streaming in crimson and in gold.
Here the laurel and the ivy spread their cups of pink and white,
And the scarlet trumpet-flower turns its clusters to the light,
While the oxydendrum's waving o'er the maiden-hair below,
And the black-haw's opal berries in the sunlight changeful glow.
Here the laurel and the ivy spread their cups of pink and white,

And the scarlet trumpet-flower turns its clusters to the light,
While the oxydendrum's waving o'er the maiden-hair below,
And the black-haw's opal berries in the sunlight changeful glow.
And she stooped and whispered softly in the red-man's list'ning ear
The secret of the valley, and its waters warm and clear;
And she told him they were flowing from her heart so warm and true,
With a wondrous gift of healing and lost vigor to renew.
And she bade him wall the hollow from which they freely welled
With giant logs of locust from her fertile bosom felled;
And thus the white man found it a hundred years ago,
When he followed Tahkeeostee in its sinuous racing flow;
As it winds among the mountains a vein from Nature's heart,
And clasps this Happy Valley unwilling to depart.

(Warm Springs, NC, August 1, 1882)

♦

Thoughts

The night is done, and the darkness
Floats like a cloud away;
While the wondrous blaze of the comet
Dies in the glare of day;

And now on the rugged mountains
I see the sunrise glow,
And catch at their base the sparkle
Of Tahkeeostee's flow;

While through the cloudy curtain
Its censer-waves uprolled
Shines a glow of green and crimson,
A gleam of autumn's gold.

And the works of man seem nothing,
Amid these gorges grand,
To the wonders wrought by Nature,
The pictures from her hand.

(Warm Springs, NC, August 14, 1882)

♦ ♦ ♦

"GO DOWN, MOSES"

Go Down, Moses

Go down, Moses
'Way down in Egypt land,
Tell ole Pharaoh,
To let my people go.

When Israel was in Egypt's land:
Let my people go,
Oppressed so hard they could not stand,
Let my people go.

Go down Moses,
'Way down in Egypt land,
Tell old Pharaoh,
To let my people go.

Then spoke the Lord, bold Moses said;
Let my people go,
If not I'll smite your first born dead,
Let my people go.

Go down, Moses,
'Way down in Egypt land,
Tell ole Pharaoh,
To let my people go.

♦ ♦ ♦

HILTON ROSS GREER (1879-1949) of Texas was a journalist
and active in cultural groups.

A Prairie Prayer

Not crouching, cloistered, upon servile knee,

With dull, down-groping eyes—

But, no less reverently,

Standing, beneath Thy searching noonday skies,

With gaze uplifted, and with soul laid bare

To the keen cleansing of Thy sun and air,

I, Lord, with free,

Full, frank, unfaltering tongue would speak with Thee:

Worn with the world, with man-made wounds a-smart,

That I might heal my heart,

To these wide prairie solitudes I fled,

Where with no roof save Heaven overhead,

Green earth my house by day, by night my bed—

I might ungyve my soul, too long unfree,

And with clear eye that did but dimly see

Through the time's trade-fogged, creed-clogged airs,

Roving fair Nature's face, not unawares

Might look on Thine, O Lord, nor blinded be;

And with tense ear might sense in Nature's tone

The deepmost underword that is Thine own.

And I have heard and seen Thee. Earth and sky,
Close confidants of spirit, ear and eye,
Noon-clear to me
Have voiced and visioned Thee most humanly.
Yea, even the least of slenderest spears that stir
Sunward finds tongue as Thine interpreter.
Blue blossom-script that stars the page I scan
In fragrant phrase proclaims God loveth Man:
And outward, lo!
Beyond all bounds the finite thought may span
Sweep these vast plains, a seeming sea that rounds
And rounds on—on-in undulations dim
Toward Earth's last, loneliest, utmost, edgemost rim!
Blue blossom-script that stars the page I scan
In fragrant phrase proclaims God loveth Man:
And outward, lo!
Beyond all bounds the finite thought may span
Sweep these vast plains, a seeming sea that rounds
And rounds on—on-in undulations dim
Toward Earth's last, loneliest, utmost, edgemost rim!
Yet this wide, awful sea has certain bounds,
Thy will has fixed, Thy hand has set them so:
Only Thy love, I know,
For Thy poor, needy kinsman, cramped below,
Thy pity for his poignant soul-distress,
Thy largeness, shaming all his littleness,
Are what these prairies seem, unbounded, limitless!

This have Thy prairies taught. And ere I go
Back to my world to bear a braver part,
Let me ensky them ever with my heart!
Nay, Lord, refashion me, reshape me so,
My soul, new-made, shall be
A prairie, broad and free,
With sun-warmed space for all humanity:
Let winds of purpose sweep it clean each morn
Of ills outworn and doubtings shadow-born:
Let faith spring lushly after storms of pain
As grasses after rain:
Let selfless aim and generous intent
Burst into blossom, rich and redolent:
Let thoughts, like teeming flocks, find large increase,
Full-rounded grow, and strong,
That from their goodly fleece
The honest weaver, Art,
May shape some rare, enduring cloth of song,
To cloak keen winter from one shrinking heart:
And, lastly, let such deep serenity
As this rapt peace of noonday fold it in
Throughout all times of tumult that may be:
Yea, make my soul a prairie, Lord. Amen.

♦ ♦ ♦

JOEL CHANDLER HARRIS (1848 - 1908) of Georgia was, of course, the author of the internationally beloved stories of "Uncle Remus." This is one of Uncle Remus's songs.

Revival Hymn

Oh, whar shill we go w'en de great day comes,
Wid de blowin' er de trumpits en de bangin' er de
drums?
How many po' sinners'll be kotched out late
En fine no latch ter de golden gate?
    No use fer ter wait twel ter-morrer!
    De sun musn't set on yo' sorrer,
    Sin's ez sharp ez a bamboo-brier—
    Oh, Lord! fetch de mo'ners up higher!

W'en de nashuns er de earf is a-stan'in all aroun',
Who's a-gwineter be choosen fer ter w'ar de glory-
crown?
Who's a-gwine fer ter stan' stiff-kneed en bol'.
En answer to der name at de callin er de roll?
    You better come now ef you comin' —
    Ole Satan is loose en a-bummin' —
    De wheels er distruckshun is a-hummin' —
    Oh, come 'long, sinner, ef you comin'!

De song er salvashun is a mighty sweet song,
En de Paradise win' blow fur en blow strong,
En Aberham's bosom, hit's soft en hit's wide,
En right dar's de place whar de sinners oughter hide!
    Oh, you nee'nter be a-stoppin en a-lookin';
    Ef you fool wid ole Satan you'll git took in;
    You'll hang on de aidge en get shook in,
    Ef you keep on a-stoppin' en a-lookin'.

De time is right now, en dish yer's de place—
Let de sun er salvashun shine squar' in yo' face;
Fight de battles er de Lord, fight soon en fight late,
En you'll allers fine a latch ter de golden gate.
    No use fer ter wait twel ter-morrer,
    De sun musn't set on yo' sorrer—
    Sin's ez sharp ez a bamboo-brier,
    Ax de Lord fer ter fetch you up higher!

♦ ♦ ♦

CHARLES WILLIAM HUBNER (1839-1929) was born in Baltimore to parents from Bavaria. He spent six years in Germany studying art, music, and classics. Returning to the U.S. he joined the Confederate Army and rose to the rank of major. After the war he became a journalist in Atlanta and published 11 books of poetry and scholarship.

To a Mocking Bird

Sweet bird! that from yon dancing spray
Dost warble forth thy varied lay,
From early morn to close of day
Melodious changes singing,
Sure thine must be the magic art
That bids my drowsy fancy start,
While from the furrows of my heart,
Hope's fairy flowers are springing.

As changeful as the sounds thy throat
Sets on the charmed winds afloat,
Till valleys near and hills remote
Attest thy peerless powers,
Have been to me the sights and scenes,
The cloudy thoughts and starry dreams,
The winter and the summer gleams,
Of life's ephemeral hours.

But all thy sad or merry lays,
Sweet bird! in thy Creator's praise
Thou pourest from the trembling sprays,
With love's delicious art;
Thus, too, will I, whate' er my fate—
In sorrow prone, or joy elate
To God my being dedicate,
And give to Him my heart.

◆ ◆ ◆

WILLIAM PRESTON JOHNSTON (1831-1899) was the son of Gen. Albert Sydney Johnston. He was a Confederate colonel who was accompanying President Davis at the time he was captured. William P. Johnston was the first president of Tulane University and a prolific speaker and writer, publishing two books of poetry, a biography of his father, and other works.

Creation

In the beginning was the Word;

It breathed its fiat, Chaos stirred;

Obedient to the First Great Cause,

It moved according to His laws,

And order reigned, design prevailed,

Nature was born, and life unveiled.

Whether our minds can grasp this plan,

Or trace the origin of man,

Why agonizing reel in doubt?

Why gibe and jeer and mock and flout

At those self-centred truths which stand

Like beacons on a desert strand?

Whether our minds can grasp this plan,

Or trace the origin of man,

Why agonizing reel in doubt?

Why gibe and jeer and mock and flout

At those self-centred truths which stand

Like beacons on a desert strand?

On each soul's consciousness they rest,
Self-evidential, and impressed
With that sharp signet, on whose face,
Deep-graved, "Necessity," we trace,
We know that like a prisoner pale,
Who from the windows of his jail
Can catch but glimpses of that world
Whose constellations are unfurled
To happier eyes which freely gaze
On all the stars in midnight's maze,
The spirit fettered here to earth
By flesh and time and space, the worth
Of realms beyond its ken can guess
Only in purblind feebleness;
But still its ample pinions feel
The power to rise and soar and wheel
And revel where the bow is bent
Which spans with hope the firmament.
Why seek our Maker in the dust,
Rather than rest in solemn trust
On that great arm able to clasp
The universe within its grasp,
And hold the balance firm and sure
While time and space and worlds endure?

What does it matter whether man
Six thousand years ago began,
Or through a myriad centuries grew,
Becoming wiser and more true?
Go, boasting skeptic, forge the links
'Twixt dust and that which knows it thinks;
Teach science to span the abyss that gapes
'Twixt man and all the race of apes;
Tell why this self-sufficing force,
Which once gave life in nature's course,
No more informs the insensate clod,
And blindly does the work of God;
Else cease thy clamorous, strident claim
That science walks thus blind and lame,
Making hypothesis the base
For all the history of our race.
Through nature's realm law reigns supreme;
Its Giver is no dotard's dream;
The universe, built with design,
Is proof of power and will divine;
And in creation, be the cause
His first or secondary laws,
By countless links this endless chain
Leads back at last to God again.

◆ ◆ ◆

"SWING LOW, SWEET CHARIOT"

Swing Low, Sweet Chariot

I ain't never been to heaven but Ah been told,
Comin' fuh to carry me home,
Dat de streets in heaben am paved with gold,
Comin' fuh to carry me home.

Swing low, sweet chariot,
Comin' fuh to carry me home,
Swing low, sweet chariot,
Comin' fuh to carry me home.

Dat ain't all, I got mo besides—
Comin' fuh to carry me home,
Ah been tuh de ribber an' Ah been baptize',
Comin' fuh to carry me home.

Swing low, sweet chariot,
Comin' fuh to carry me home,
Swing low, sweet chariot,
Comin' fuh to carry me home.

Lemme tell yuh whut's a mattah o' fac
Comin' fuh to carry me home,
Ef yuh each leaves de debbil, you nevah go back
Comin' fuh to carry me home.

Swing low, sweet chariot,
Comin' fuh to carry me home,
Swing low, sweet chariot,
Comin' fuh to carry me home.

Yuh see dem sisters dress so fine?
Comin' fuh to carry me home,
Well, dey ain't got Jesus on dey min',
Comin' fuh to carry me home.

Swing low, sweet chariot,
Comin' fuh to carry me home,
Swing low, sweet chariot,
Comin' fuh to carry me home.

Ef salvation wuz a thing money could buy,
Comin' fuh to carry me home,
Den de rich would live an' de po' would die.
Comin' fuh to carry me home.

Swing low, sweet chariot,
Comin' fuh to carry me home,
Swing low, sweet chariot,
Comin' fuh to carry me home.

But Ah'm so glad God fix it so,
Comin' fuh to carry me home.
Dat de rich mus' die jes' as well as de po'!
Comin' fuh to carry me home,

Swing low, sweet chariot,
Comin' fuh to carry me home,
Swing low, sweet chariot,
Comin' fuh to carry me home.

◆ ◆ ◆

JOHN BANISTER TABB (1845-1909) of Virginia was too young and weak of eyesight to join the Confederate army. As a mere youth he enlisted on blockade runners and made 23 voyages. On the last he was captured and imprisoned at Point Lookout, Maryland, where he became friends with fellow prisoner Sidney Lanier. After the war, Tabb became a Roman Catholic priest and a professor of English. He spent his later years in complete blindness.

Evolution

Out of the dusk a shadow,

Then, a spark;

Out of the cloud a silence,

Then, a lark;

Out of the heart a rapture,

Then, a pain;

Out of the dead, cold ashes,

Life again.

♦

Kildee

Kildee! Kildee! Far o'er the lea
At twilight comes the cry.
Kildee! A marsh-mate answereth
Across the shallow sky.
Kildee! Kildee! thrills over me
A rhapsody of light,
As star to star gives utterance
Between the day and night.
Kildee! Kildee! O Memory,
The twin birds, Joy and Pain,
Like shadows parted by the sun,
At twilight meet again!

♦ ♦ ♦

LEONARD CHARLES *VAN OPPEN* (1868-1935) of North Carolina was born in Holland and raised in North Carolina. He was a poet, translator of European literature into English, and author of many articles in the leading journals of the day. In World War I, he was a naval officer said to be involved in secret work.

Evolution

A young ape, who, aspiring to be man,

Had studied evolution, humbly came

To see a wise gorilla of great fame;

And begged that old philosopher to scan

His graduating thesis, which began,

With some attempt at beauty, to acclaim

Those various virtues which the poets name

As the divine prerogatives of man.

"But to be human," said the sage, with passion,

"Is, since the war, no longer here the fashion.

Why should an ape aspire to be a man?

It is the law that evolution ends

As it begins. Man who as ape began

Now through the tiger to the ape descends."

♦ ♦ ♦

MORTON BRYAN WHARTON, D.D. (1839-1908) was a prominent Baptist minister who served in pulpits all over the South and was the author of numerous popular books about the Bible. In the Confederate army he assisted chaplains. He was born in Virginia but lived primarily in Eufaula, Alabama, and was well-educated and travelled in Europe. His poem illustrates the usual friendly relations between Christian denominations in the South. Wharton's verse also appears in vol. 3 of *The Land They Loved.*

The Denominational Team

A rustic teamster on the street

Of a Texas town appears,

He brings the people to their feet,

They stand in wonderment complete,

For the names he called his steers.

"Get up, get up there, Methodist;

Whoa, Baptist!" loud he cries.

He gives his whip a lightning twist,

Old Presbyterian's barely missed,

To "Campbellite" it flies.

"Pray tell us what your names may mean?"

Exclaimed a wag who passed;

The man replied, "Each steer, I ween,

Does to some sect of Christians lean,

And so I've got them classed."

"Just look at Methodist," he said;
"He goes at a rapid pace,
He bellows till he splits your head;
But once neglected to be fed
He's sure to fall from grace.

"Episcopalian's kind and bright,
But gay and giddy ever,
While the reverse is Campbellite;
He's always spoiling for a fight,
And lies down in the river.

"There's Presbyterian, strict new school,
Has hydrophobia sorter,
He's true and faithful as a rule,
But when he strikes a stream or pool
He leaps clean o'er the water.

"There's Baptist, good, but very queer,
On charity he's off;
He's willing and obedient e'er,
But won't permit another steer
To eat from out his trough.

"That big fat ox is Catholic;

He's of most ancient birth;

He's up to many a crafty trick,

Against all other steers will kick,

And always wants the earth.

"But though these steers are different quite,

At one great end they aim;

'Tis true they sometimes skuik and fight,

But still they keep the goal in sight,

And get there all the same."

♦ ♦ ♦

Folk Songs

"ARKANSAS TRAVELER"

Arkansas Traveler

"Hey, old man, why don't you cover your house?"
Well, it's a-raining."
"Why don't you cover it when it's not a-raining?"
"Well, it don't need it then."

"Hey, old man, how far ... where does this road go to?"
"Well, I've been living here twenty years, and it's not gone
anywhere yet."

"Hey, old man, how far is it to Little Rock?"
"Well, I don't know how far it is to Little Rock,
but there's a hell of a big rock down here in Paul's field."

"Hey, old man, what's the idea for having just three
chickens here?"
"Well, it takes two to hold up the rock while the other'n
gets the worm."

"Hey, old man, head that cow."
"Well, she's headed."
"I mean, speak to her."
"Howdy, cow."

"I mean, speak to her."

"Howdy, cow."

"I mean, turn her."

"Well, the hairy side's out."

"Hey, old man, can you ford this creek?"

"Yeah, I guess you can; ducks and geese do."

"Hey, old man, how did your taters turn out?"

"Well, they didn't turn out. Me and Sal had to dig 'em out."

"Hey, old man, what caused that corn to be so yellow?"

"Well, we planted the yellow kind."

"Well, it looks like you just got a half a crop here."

"Well, all I intend to have. The landlord gets the other half

♦ ♦ ♦

"THE BOLL WEEVIL SONG"

The Boll Weevil Song

Oh, de boll weevil am a little black bug,
Come from Mexico, dey say,
Come all de way to Texas,
    jus' a-lookin' foh a place to stay,
Jus' a-lookin' foh a home,
    jus' a-lookin' foh a home.

De first time I seen de boll weevil,
He was settin' on de square.
De next time I seen de boll weevil,
    he had all of his family dere.
Jus' a-lookin' foh a home,
    jus' a-lookin' foh a home.

De farmer say to de weevil:
"What make yo' head so red?"
De weevil say to de farmer,
    "It's a wondah I ain't dead,
A-lookin' foh a home,
    jus' a-lookin' foh a home."

De farmer take de boll weevil,
An' he put him in de hot san'.
De weevil say: "Dis is mighty hot,
      but I'll stan' it like a man,
Dis'll be my home, it'll be my home."

De farmer take de boll weevil,
An' he put him in a lump of ice;
De weevil say to de farmer:
      "Dis is mighty cool and nice,
It'll be my home, dis'll be my home."

De farmer take de boll weevil,
An' he put him in de fire.
De boll weevil say to de farmer:
      "Here I are, here I are,
Dis'll be my home, dis'll be my home."

De boll weevil say to de farmer:
"You better leave me alone;
I done eat all yo' cotton,
      now I'm goin' to start on yo corn,
I'll have a home, I'll have a home.

De merchant got half de cotton,
De boll weevil got de res'.
Didn't leave de farmer's wife
      but one ole cotton dress,
An' it's full of holes, it's full of holes.

De farmer say to de merchant:
"We's in an awful fix;
De boll weevil et all de cotton up
        and lef us only sticks,
We's got no home, we's got no home."

De farmer say to de merchant:
"We ain't made but only one bale,
And befoh we'll give yo' dat one we'll fight and go
to jail,
We'll have a home, we'll have a home."

An' if anybody should ax you
Who it was dat make dis song,
Jus' tell 'em 'twas a big buck niggah
        wid a paih o' blue duckin's on,
Ain't got no home, ain't got no home.

♦ ♦ ♦

"CLAUDE ALLEN"

(This is based upon a real event—a shootout in the Hillsville, Virginia courthouse in 1912. Many thought that Allen's execution was unjust and politically motivated. The story is told in Thomas Moore's book, *No Villains, No Heroes*.)

Claude Allen

Claude Allen, he and his dear old pappy
Have met their fatal doom at last.
Their friends are glad their trouble's ended
And hope their souls are now at rest.

Claude Allen was that tall and handsome,
He still had hopes until the end
That he'll some way or other
Escape his death at the Richmond pen.

The governor being so hard-hearted,
Not caring what his friends might say,
He finally took his sweet life from him.
In the cold, cold ground his body lay.

Claude Allen had a pretty sweetheart,
She mourned the loss of the one she loved.
She hoped to meet beyond the river,
Her fair young face in heaven above.

Claude's mother's tears were gently flowing,
All for the one she loved so dear.
It seemed no one could tell her troubles,
It seemed no one could tell but her.

How sad, how sad, to think of killin'
A man all in his youthful years,
A-leaving his old mother weepin'
And all his friends in bitter tears.

Look up on yonder lonely mountain,
Claude Allen sleeps beneath the clay.
No more you'll hear his words of mercy
Or see his face till Judgment Day.

Come all young boys, you may take warning.
Be careful how you go astray,
Or you might be like poor Claude Allen
And have this awful debt to pay.

♦ ♦ ♦

"THE DYING COWBOY"

The Dying Cowboy

"O bury me not on the lone prairie,"
These words came low and mournfully
From the pallid lips of a youth who lay
On his dying bed at the close of day.

He had wailed in pain till o'er his brow
Death's shadows fast were gathering now;
He thought of his home and his loved ones nigh
As the cowboys gathered to see him die.

"O bury me not on the lone prairie
Where the wild cayotes will howl o'er me,
In a narrow grave just six by three,
O bury me not on the lone prairie.

"In fancy I listen to the well known words
Of the free, wild winds and the song of the birds;
I think of home and the cottage in the bower
And the scenes I loved in my childhood's hour.

"It matters not, I've oft been told,
Where the body lies when the heart grows cold;
Yet grant, oh grant this wish to me,
O bury me not on the lone prairie.

"O bury me not on the lone prairie,
In a narrow grave six foot by three,
Where the buffalo paws o'er a prairie sea,
O bury me not on the lone prairie.

"I've always wanted to be laid when
I died In the little churchyard on the green hillside;
By my father's grave, there let mine be,
And bury me not on the lone prairie.

"Let my death slumber be where my mother's prayer
And a sister's tear will mingle there,
Where my friends can come and weep o'er me;
O bury me not on the lone prairie.

"O bury me not on the lone prairie
In a narrow grave just six by three,
Where the buzzard waits and the wind blows free;
Then bury me not on the lone prairie.

"There is another whose tears may be shed
For one who lies on a prairie bed;
It pained me then and it pains me now;
She has curled these locks, she has kissed this brow.

"These locks she has curled, shall the rattlesnake kiss?
This brow she has kissed, shall the cold grave press?
For the sake of the loved ones that will weep for me
O bury me not on the lone prairie.

    "O bury me not on the lone prairie
    Where the wild cayotes will howl o'er me,
    Where the blizzard beats and the wind goes free,
    O bury me not on the lone prairie.

"O bury me not," and his voice failed there,
But we took no heed of his dying prayer;
In a narrow grave just six by three
We buried him there on the lone prairie,

Where the dew-drops glow and the butterflies rest,
and the flowers bloom o'er the prairie's crest;
Where the wild cayote and winds sport free
On a wet saddle blanket lay a cowboy-ee.

    "O bury me not on the lone prairie;
    Where the wild cayotes will howl o'er me,
    Where the rattlesnakes hiss and the crow flies free
    O bury me not on the lone prairie."

O we buried him there on the lone prairie
Where the wild rose blooms and the wind blows free,
O his pale young face nevermore to see,—
For we buried him there on the lone prairie.

Yes, we buried him there on the lone prairie
Where the owl all night hoots mournfully,
And the blizzard beats and the winds blow free
O'er his lonely grave on the lone prairie.

And the cowboys now as they roam the plain,—
For they marked the spot where his bones were lain,—
Fling a handful of roses o'er his grave,
With a prayer to Him who his soul will save.

"O bury me not on the lone prairie
Where the wolves can howl and growl o'er me;
Fling a handful of roses o'er my grave.
With a prayer to Him who my soul will save."

♦ ♦ ♦

"JESSE JAMES WAS HIS NAME"

Jesse James Was His Name

Jesse James Was His Name
He robbed the Glendale train,
He stole from the rich and he gave to the poor,
He'd a hand and a heart and a brain.

Well it was Robert Ford, that dirty little coward,
I wonder how he feels,
For he ate of Jesse's bread and he slept in Jesse's bed,
And he laid poor Jesse in his grave.

Well Jesse had a wife to mourn for his life,
Three children, they were brave,
Well that dirty little coward that shot Mister Howard,
He laid poor Jesse in his grave.

Jesse was a man, a friend to the poor,
He'd never rob a mother or a child,
There never was a man with the law in his hand,
That could take Jesse James alive.

Jesse was a man, a friend to the poor,
He'd never see a man suffer pain,
And with his brother Frank he robbed the Chicago bank,
And stopped the Glendale train.

It was on a Saturday night and the moon was shining bright,
They robbed the Glendale train,
 And people they did say o'er many miles away
It was those outlaws, they're Frank and Jesse James

Now the people held their breath when they heard of
    Jesse's death,
And wondered how he ever came to fall
Robert Ford, it was a fact, he shot Jesse in the back
While Jesse hung a picture on the wall

Now Jesse went to rest with his hand on his breast,
The devil will be upon his knee.
He was born one day in the County Clay,
And he came from a solitary race.

Well Jesse had a wife to mourn for his life,
Three children, they were brave,
Well that dirty little coward that shot Mister Howard,
He laid poor Jesse in his grave.

♦ ♦ ♦

ROSA LeCARSON

(In 1913 in Atlanta Leo Frank murdered 13-year-old Mary Phagan. The event created a number of folk songs that were sung at public gatherings. This is a late and milder version by **Rosa LeCarson** (1909-1992), the first popular and the first recorded female country music artist.

Little Mary Phagan

Little Mary Phagan, she went to town one day

She went to the pencil fact'ry, to get her little pay

She left her home at eleven, when she kissed her mother good-bye

Not one time did the po' child think, she was goin' right to die

Leo Frank met her, with a blues we hardly know

He smiled and said, "Lil' Mary, now you go home no mo'"

He sneaked along behind her, 'til she reached the little room

He laughed and said, "Lil' Mary, you met your fatal doom."

She fell upon her knees, to Leo Frank she pled

Because she was virtuous, he hit her across the head

The tears rolled down her rosy cheeks, the blood flowed down
    her back

She remembered tellin' her mother what time she would be back

He killed lil' Mary Phagan, was on one holiday

Then called for ol' Jim Conley to take her body away

He took her to the basement, bound hand and feet

Down in the basement, lil' Mary lay asleep

♦ ♦ ♦

Newt Lee was the watchman, when he went to wind the key
Down in the basement, lil' Mary he could see
He called for the officers, their names I do not know
They came to the pencil fact'ry, saying, "Newt Lee, you must go."

They took him to the jailhouse, locked him in a cell
The poor ol' innocent nigger, knew nothin' for to tell
I have a notion in my head, when Frank comes to die
He took his damnation in the courthouse in the sky

The astonished asked the question, the angels they do say
Why he kill lil' Mary, upon one holiday?
Come all of you good people, wherever you may be,
Supposin' little Mary belonged to you or me?

Her mother sets a-weepin'
She weeps and mourns all day
She prays to meet her baby
In a better world some day

Judge Roan passed the sentence
You bet he passed it well
Solicitor Hugh M. Dorsey
Sent Leo Frank to ----

♦ ♦ ♦

"THE KNOXVILLE GIRL"

The Knoxville Girl

In the town of Knoxville I used to live and dwell,
And in that town of Knoxville I owned a flour mill.

I fell in love with a Knoxville girl, with dark and rolling eyes,
I promised her I'd marry her if me she'd ne'er deny.

I called her at her sister's house, about nine o'clock at night,
And little did that fair girl think I owned her in a fright.

I said to her, "Let's take a walk and view the meadows gay,
That we might have a little talk and plan our wedding day."

We walked along, we talked along, till we came to level ground.
There I picked up an edgewood stick and I knocked that fair girl down.

She fell upon her bended knee. "Oh Lord, have mercy!" she cried.
"Oh, Willie, dear, don't murder me here. I'm not prepared to die."

Not minding one word she said, I beat her more and more.
I beat her till the ground around stood in a bloody gore.

I took her by her long yellow hair, I dragged her round and round.
I dragged her to still waters deep that flows through Knoxville town.

I called at my mother's house about twelve o'clock that night,
And Mother, being worried, got up all in a fright,

Saying, "Son, oh son, what have you don't to bloody your hands
    and clothes?"
I answered to my mother's request, "Been bleeding at the nose."

I called for a candle to light myself to bed,
And also for a handkerchief to bind my aching head.

I rolled and tumbled the livelong night. Nothing could I see,
Nothing but the flames of hell a-sweeping over me.

About six weeks or later that Knoxville girl was found,
A-floating down still waters that flows through Knoxville town.

Her sister swore my life away, she swore without a doubt
That I must be the very lad that took her sister out.

And now they're going to hang me, a death I hate to die,
They're going to hang me up so high between the earth and sky.

♦ ♦ ♦

"TOM DOOLEY"

(Thomas C. Dula was accused of the murder of Laura Foster in Wilkes County, North Carolina, in 1866. He was convicted in two controversial trials and was hanged in 1868 protesting his innocence. The song exists in several versions and became a "folk music" hit by the Kingston Trio almost a century later.)

Tom Dooley

Hang your head Tom Dooley

Hang your head and cry

Killed poor Laura Foster

And you know you're bound to die

You took her on the hillside

And begged to be excused

You took her on the hillside

The Hid her clothes and shoes

You dug her grave four feet wide

Dug it three feet deep

Rolled the cold clay over her

And tromped it with your feet

Hang your head Tom Dooley

Hang your head and cry

Killed poor Laura Foster

And you know you're bound to die

Took her on the hillside
Stabbed with a knife
Took her on the hillside
And then you took her life

Trouble, oh it's trouble
A-rollin' through my breast
As long as I'm a-livin', boys
They ain't a-gonna let me rest

Hang your head Tom Dooley
Hang your head and cry
Killed poor Laura Foster
And you know you're bound to die

This time tomorrow morning
Where do you reckon I'll be
Down in some lonesome valley
Just swinging from a white oak tree

You can take down my old violin
And play it all you please
For at this time tomorrow morning
It'll be of no use to me

Hang your head Tom Dooley
Hang your head and cry
Killed poor Laura Foster
And you know you're bound to die

I know they're gonna hang me
Tomorrow I'll be dead
Though I never even harmed a hair
On poor little Laurie's head

In this world and one more
Then reckon where I'll be
If it wasn't for Sheriff Grayson
I'd be in Tennessee

Hang your head Tom Dooley
Hang your head and cry
Killed poor Laura Foster
And you know you're bound to die

◆ ◆ ◆

"WILDWOOD FLOWER"

(This is merely a representative example of the rich folk music written or collected by A.P. Carter in the Appalachians in the early 20th century.)

Wildwood Flower

Oh, I'll twine with my mingles and waving black hair

With the roses so red and the lilies so fair

And the myrtle so bright with the emerald hue

The pale and the leader and eyes look like blue

Oh I'll dance, I will sing and my laugh shall be gay

I will charm every heart, in his crown I will sway

When I woke from my dreaming, my idol was clay

All portion of love had all flown away

Oh he taught me to love him and promised to love

And to cherish me over all others above

How my heart is now wond'ring no mis'ry can tell

He's left me no warning, no words of farewell

Oh, he taught me to love him and called me his flower

That was blooming to cheer him through life's dreary hour

Oh, I long to see him and regret the dark hour

He's gone and neglected this pale wildwood flower

◆ ◆ ◆

"THE WRECK ON THE C. & O."

(This song refers to a real event near Hinton, Virginia, in 1890. The F.F.V. was the "Fast Flying Vestibule.")

The Wreck on the C. & O.

A-long came the F. F. V, the fastest on the line,

A-running o'er the C. and O. Road, twenty minutes behind the time,

A-running into Sewall yard, was quartered on the line,

A-waiting for strict orders and in the cab to ride.

Chorus:

Man-y a man's been murdered by the railroad, railroad.

Man-y a man's been murdered by the railroad,

    And laid in his lonesome grave.

And when she blew for Hinton, her engineer was there

George Alley was his name, with bright and wavery hair;

His fireman, Jack Dixon, was standing by his side,

Awaiting for strict orders and in the cab to ride.

George Alley's mother came to him with a basket on her arm,

She handed him a letter, saying, "Be careful how you run;

And if you run your engine right, you'll get there just on time."

For many a man has lost his life in trying to make lost time."

George Alley said, "Dear mother, your letter I'll take heed.

I know my engine is all right and I know that she will speed;

So o'er this road I mean to run with a speed unknown to all,
And when I blow for Clifton Forge, they'll surely hear my call."

George Alley said to his fireman, "Jack, a little extra steam;
I intend to run old No. 4 the fastest ever seen;
So o'er this road I mean to fly like angels' wings unfold,
And when I blow for the Big Bend Tunnel, they'll surely hear my call."

George Alley said to his fireman, "Jack, a rock ahead I see,
And I know that death is lurking there for to grab both you and me;
So from this cab, dear Jack, you leap, your darling life to save,
For I want you to be an engineer while I'm sleeping in my grave."

"Oh no, dear George! that will not do, I want to die with you."
"Oh no, dear Jack! that will not be, I'll die for you and me."
So from the cab dear Jack did leap, old New River was running high,
And he kissed the hand of darling George as No. 4 flew by.

So in the cab dear George did leap, the throttle he did pull;
Old No. 4 just started off, like a mad and angry bull.

So up the road she dashed; against the rock she crashed;
The engine turning over and the coaches they came last;
George Alley's head in the firebox lay, while the burning
    flames rolled o'er;
"I'm glad I was born an engineer, to die on the C. & O. Road."

George Alley's mother came to him and in sorrow she did sigh,
When she looked upon her darling boy and saw that he must die.
"Too late, too late, dear mother! my doom is almost o'er,
And I know that God will let me in when I reach that golden shore."

The doctor said, "Dear George, O darling boy, keep still;
Your life may yet be spared, if it is God's blessed will."
"Oh no, dear Doc, that can not be, I want to die so free,
I want to die on the engine I love, 143."

The people came from miles around this engineer to see.
George Alley said, "God bless you, friends, I am sure you
      will find me here."
His head and face all covered with blood, his eyes you could not see,
And as he died he cried aloud, "O near, my God, to Thee!"

♦ ♦ ♦

Home

(WILLIAM) HERVEY ALLEN (1889-1949) came from a prominent Pittsburgh family. He was a combat infantry officer in World War I and wrote what is considered a classic war memoir, *Toward the Fire*. After the war Allen lived in Charleston until 1925. He and Charleston were mutually sympatico. He was active in the Poetry Society of South Carolina and in the local writer community. His verse during this period, published in 1921, was concerned entirely with the South Carolina Lowcountry. After leaving Charleston Allen wrote *Anthony Adverse*, which became a best-seller and movie, and other laudable novels.

La Fayette Lands

That evening, gathered on the vessel's poop,

They saw the glimmering land,

And far lights moved there,

As once Columbus saw them, winking, strange;

Around the ship two darkies in a small canoe

Paddled and grinned, and held up silver fish.

Over the high ship's tumble-home

A pinnace slid,

Slow, lowered from the squealing davit-ropes,

And from a port a-square with lantern light,

The little, leather trunks were passed,

Ironbound and quaint; while down the vessel's side

With voluble advice, *bon voyage* and *au revoir*,

The chatting Frenchmen came—

Click-clap of rapiers clipping on hard boots,

Cocked hats and merry eyes.

The great ship backs its yards,
With drooping sails, await,
A spider-web of spars and lantern-lights,
While like a pilot shark, the slim canoe,
A V-shaped ripple wrinkling from its jaws,
Slides noiselessly across the swells,
Leading the swinging boat's crew to the beach;
And all the world slides up—
And then the stars slide down—
As ocean breathes; while evening falls,
And destiny is being rowed ashore.

The twilight-muffled bells of town, the bark of dogs,
The distant shouts, and smell of burning wood,
Fall graciously upon their sea-tired sense.
Wide-trousered, barefoot sailors carry them to land,
Tho snake-voiced waves flaunt frothing up the beach;
The horse-hide trunks are piled upon a dune;
And there a little Frenchman takes his stand,
Hawk-faced and ardent,
While his brown cloak droops about him
Like young falcon plumes.

Gray beach, gray twilight, and gray sea—
How strange the scrub palmettoes down the coast!
No purple-castled heights, like dear Auvergne,
Against the background of the Puy de Dome,

But land as level as the sea, a sandy road
That twists through myrtle thickets
Where the black boys lead.
Far down a moss-draped avenue of oaks
Far down a moss-draped avenue of oaks
There is a flash of torches, and the lights
Go flitting past the bottle panes;
A cracked plantation bell dull-clangs;
The beagles bay,
Black faces swarm, with ivory eyeballs glazed—
Court dwarfs that served thick chocolate, on their knees
In damasked, perfumed rooms at grand Versailles,
Were all the blacks the French had ever seen.

Major Huger, lace-ruffled shirt, knee-breeks,
A saddle-pistol in his hand, Waits on the terrace,
Ready for "hospitality" to British privateers;
But now no London accent takes his ears,
No English bow so low, "Good evening, sair;
I am de la Fayette, and these, monsieur,
My friends, and this, le Baron Kalb."

Welcome's the custom of the time and land—
And these are noblemen of France!
Now is Bartholomew for turkeycocks,
Old wines decant, the chandeliers flare up,
The slave row brims with lights;
And horses gallop off to summon guests.

After the ship--how good the spacious rooms!
How strange mosquito canopies on beds!
Knights of St. Louis sniff the frying yams,
Venison, and turtle,—
The old green turtle died tonight—
The children's eyes grow wider on the stairs.

Down in the library,
The Marquis, writing back to old Auvergne,
Has sanded down the ink;
Again the quill pen squeaks:
"A ship will sail tomorrow back to France,
By special providence for you, dear wife;
Tonight there will be toasts to Washington,
To our good Louis and his Antoinette—
There will be toasts tonight for la Fayette...."
He melts the wax;
Look, how the candle gutters at the flame!
And now he seals the letter with his ring.

♦

Marsh Tackies

Browsing on the salty marsh grass,
Barrel-ribbed and blowsy-bellied,
With a neigh as shrill as whistles
And their mouths red-raw from thistles,
I have seen the brown marsh tackies,
Hiding in the swamps at Kiawah,
With the gray mosquito patches
Gory on their shaggy thatches.
Balky, vicious, and degenerates,
They are small as Spanish jennets,
But their sires were with El Tarab,
When he conquered Andalusia
For the Prophet and the Arab;
And they came with Ponce de Leon,
When the Spaniard made a peon
And a Christian of the Carib.
Peering from palmetto thickets
At some fort's coquina wickets,
Startled Indians saw them grazing,
Thunder-stamping and amazing
As the beasts from other stars,
When they galloped down savannas,
And their masters seemed centaurs
With the new white metal blazing.

Thus they came, these little beasts,
With the men-at-arms and priests,
In the west with Coronado
When he reached the Colorado,
In the east with bold De Soto
In the search for El Dorado,
And they packed the bells and toys
That the chieftains loved like boys;
Struggling through the swamps and briars
After dons and tonsured friars;
Dying in the forests dismal,
Till the shrill of silver clarion
Brought the buzzards to the carrion
Round the smoke of lonely fires
In a continent abysmal.

So De Soto left them dying,
Heedless of their human crying;
Here he turned them loose to die
Underneath a foreign sky;
But they lived on thicket dross,
On the leaves and Spanish moss—
And I wonder, and I wonder,
When I hear the startled thunder
Of their hoofs die down the reaches
Of these Carolina beaches.

♦

Carolina Spring Song

Against the swart magnolias' sheen
Pronged maples, like a stag's new horn,
Stand gouted red upon the green,
In March when shaggy buds are shorn.

Then all a mist-streaked, sunny day
The long sea-islands lean to hear
A water harp that shallows play
To lull the beaches' fluted ear.

When this same music wakes the gift
Of pregnant beauty in the sod,
And makes the uneasy vultures shift
Like evil things afraid of God,

Then, then it is I love to drift
Upon the flood-tide's lazy swirls,
While from the level rice fields lift
The spiritu'ls of darky girls.

I hear them singing in the fields
Like voices from the long-ago;
They speak to me of somber worlds
And sorrows that the humble know;

Of sorrow-yet their tones release
A harmony of larger hours
From easy epochs long at peace
Amid an irony of flowers.

So if they sometimes seem a choir
That cast a chill of doubt on spring,
They have still higher notes of fire
Like cardinals upon the wing.

◆ ◆ ◆

JOHN HENRY BONER (1845-1903) was alienated from his native North Carolina as a Republican journalist and office-holder.

The Wanderer Back Home

Back in the Old North State,
Back to the place of his birth,
Back through the pines' colonnaded gate
To the dearest spot on earth.
No sweeter joy can a star feel
When into the sky it thrills
Than the rapture that wings a Tar Heel
Come back to his native hills.

From coast to mountain heights
Old North Carolina lies,
A cornucopia of delights
Under her summer skies,
And autumn gives rich treasure
To the overflowing horn,
Adding a juicy measure
Of grape and rye and corn.

In June a tree so fragrant
Scents the delicious air
That busiest bees grow vagrant
And doze in its blossoms fair.
"Persimmons!" the wanderer cries;
And along time's frosted track
The luscious purple fruit he spies,
And boyhood's days drift back!

With fall comes the burst of the cartridge;
The squirrel and the rabbit are his;
Down tumbles the whirring partridge,
And the cook makes the wild duck sizz;
But for these not so much does he care,
No matter how dainty the caters;
Just seat him fair in an old splint chair
And give him possum and taters.

♦ ♦ ♦

GEORGE GRAHAM CURRIE (1867-1926) was born in Canada and settled in West Palm Beach, Florida, in 1895. He was a lawyer, banker, and civic booster who became known as the Poet Laureate of Florida.

Florida My Home

Eternal Summerland! To thee
My dragging mem'ry strays,
To revel near thy Southern sea
And stretch my honeyed days;
Thy silv'ry springs, thy silent streams
Are mirrored on my heart
Tho' far I toil, my faithful dreams
Refuse from thee to part.

I love each lake and evergreen
From Suwannee to the Keys,
I love each piney woodland scene
E'en wastes of sand can please;
Romance and legend win applause
For many a mound and glade;
While sentiment fills ev'ry pause
Thy mocking birds have made.

Sweet land of flow'rs and whisp'ring palms,
Of oleanders fair,
Thy fragrance and thy healing balms
Relieve me of my care;
Pill all forgot the fleeting years
And aging limbs uncouth;
De Leon's quest in thee appears—
Thou bourne of endless youth!

What matter if mere wealth takes wing;—
To live is riches there.
The luscious fruits thy gardens bring
Are feasts the gods might share.
I need not fear the Northern blast
When thro' thy groves I roam;
So take me back for aye to rest
In Florida, my home.

♦ ♦ ♦

(EDWIN) DUBOSE HEYWARD (1885—1940) of Charleston is famous for his novel of black Charleston life, *Porgy* 1925. These early verses are from 1921 or before.

Dusk

They tell me she is beautiful, my City,

That she is colorful and quaint, alone

Among the cities. But I, I who have known

Her tenderness, her courage, and her pity,

Have felt her forces mould me, mind and bone,

Life after life, up from her first beginning.

How can I think of her in wood and stone!

To others she has given of her beauty,

Her gardens, and her dim, old, faded ways,

Her laughter, and her happy, drifting hours,

Glad, spendthrift April, squandering her flowers,

The sharp, still wonder of her Autumn days;

Her chimes that shimmer from St. Michael's steeple

Across the deep maturity of June,

Like sunlight slanting over open water

Under a high, blue, listless afternoon.

But when the dusk is deep upon the harbor,

She finds me where her rivers meet and speak,

And while the constellations ride the silence

High overhead, her cheek is on my cheek.

I know her in the thrill behind the dark
When sleep brims all her silent thoroughfares.
She is the glamor in the quiet park
That kindles simple things like grass and trees.
She is the glamor in the quiet park
That kindles simple things like grass and trees.
Wistful and wanton as her sea-born airs,
Bringer of dim, rich, age-old memories.
Out on the gloom-deep water, when the nights
Are choked with fog, and perilous, and blind,
She is the faith that tends the calling lights.
Hers is the stifled voice of harbor bells
Muffled and broken by the mist and wind.
Hers are the eyes through which I look on life
And find it brave and splendid.
And the stir Of hidden music shaping all my songs,
And these my songs, my all, belong to her.

♦

Modern Philosopher

They fight your battles for you every day,
The zealous ones, who sorrow in your life.
Undaunted by a century of strife,
With urgent fingers still they point the way
To drawing rooms, in decorous array,
And moral Heavens where no casual wife
May share your lot; where dice and ready knife
Are barred; and feet are silent when you pray.

But you have music in your shuffling feet,
And spirituals for a lenient Lord,
Who lets you sing your promises away.
You hold your sunny corner of the street,
And pluck deep beauty from a banjo chord:
Philosopher whose future is today!

◆ ◆ ◆

JUDD MORTIMER LEWIS (1867-1945) of Texas was a Houston journalist and the first Poet Laureate of Texas.

Longing For Texas (1903)

No, it isn't hot in Texas; and the cool night dews are falling,
And the katydids are chirping in the grass beside the pool;
And from out the moonlit distances the mocking-birds are calling,
And I know the days are hazy and the nights perfumed and cool.

And I know the jasmine's blooming as it bloomed in all its whiteness,
And my heart is heavy in me for I'm far away today,
And my spirit lags forever, and my tread has lost its lightness,
And I'm humming "Down in Dixie," and my heart throbs: "Look away!"

Oh, it isn't hot in Texas, for the cool gulf breeze is blowing,
And the cattle all are standing underneath the wide oak trees,
Or are wending slowly homeward from the pasture, lowing, lowing;
And a drone comes softly to me from the honey-laden bees.

And I'm longing, longing, longing for the day of my home-coming,
For the lowing of the cattle and the shadows on the stream,
For the mocking-bird's far calling, and the laden bees' soft humming,
And the night-dews falling coolly as the shadows in a dream.

Oh, the rolling, rolling prairies, and the grasses waving, waving
Like green billows neath the gulf breeze in the perfumed, purple gloam!
Oh, my heart is heavy, heavy, and my eyes are craving, craving,
For the fertile plains and forests of my far-off Texas home.

♦ ♦ ♦

JOHN CHARLES McNEILL (1874-1907) was a Poet Laureate of North Carolina.

Away Down Home

'T will not be long before they hear
The bullbat on the hill,
And in the valley through the dusk
The pastoral whippoorwill.
A few more friendly suns will call
The bluets through the loam
And star the lanes with buttercups
Away down home.

"Knee-deep!" from reedy places
Will sing the river frogs.
The terrapins will sun themselves
On all the jutting logs.
The angler's cautious oar will leave
A trail of drifting foam
Along the shady currents
Away down home.

The mocking-bird will feel again
The glory of his wings,
And wanton through the balmy air
And sunshine while he sings,

With a new cadence in his call,
The glint-wing'd crow will roam
From field to newly-furrowed field
Away down home.

When dogwood blossoms mingle
With the maple's modest red,
And sweet arbutus wakes at last
From out her winter's bed,
'T would not seem strange at all to meet
A dryad or a gnome,
Or Pan or Psyche in the woods
Away down home.

Then come with me, thou weary heart!
Forget thy brooding ills,
Since God has come to walk among
His valleys and his hills!
The mart will never miss thee,
Nor the scholar's dusty tome,
And the Mother waits to bless thee,
Away down home.

◆

Jesse Covington

If I have had some merry times
In roaming up and down the earth,
Have made some happy-hearted rhymes
And had my brimming share of mirth,
And if this song should live in fame
When my brief day is dead and gone,
Let it recall with mine the name
Of old man Jesse Covington.

Let it recall his waggish heart—
Yeke-hey, yeke-hey, hey-diddle-diddle
When, while the fire-logs fell apart,
He snatched the bow across his fiddle,
And looked on, with his eyes half shut,
Which meant his soul was wild with fun,
At our mad capers through the hut
Of old man Jesse Covington.

For all the thrilling tales he told,
For all the tunes the fiddle knew,
For all the glorious nights of old
We boys and he have rollicked through,
For laughter all unknown to wealth
That roared responsive to a pun,
A hale, ripe age and ruddy health
To old man Jesse Covington!

♦

"97": The Fast Mail

Where the rails converge to the station yard
She stands one moment, breathing hard,

And then, with a snort and a clang of steel,
She settles her strength to the stubborn wheel,

And out, through the tracks that lead astray,
Cautiously, slowly she picks her way,

And gathers her muscle and guards her nerve,
When she swings her nose to the westward curve,

And takes the grade, which slopes to the sky,
With a bound of speed and a conquering cry.

The hazy horizon is all she sees,
Nor cares for the meadows, stirred with bees,

Nor the long, straight stretches of silent land,
Nor the ploughman, that shades his eye with his hand,

Nor the cots and hamlets that know no more
Than a shriek and a flash and a flying roar;

But, bearing her tidings, she trembles and throbs,
And laughs in her throat, and quivers and sobs;

And the fire in her heart is a red core of heat,
That drives like a passion through forest and street,

Till she sees the ships in their harbor at rest,
And sniffs at the trail to the end of her quest.

If I were the driver who handles her reins,
Up hill and down hill and over the plains,

To watch the slow mountains give back in the west,
To know the new reaches that wait every crest,

To hold, when she swerves, with a confident clutch,
And feel how she shivers and springs to the touch,

With the snow on her back and the sun in her face,
And nothing but time as a quarry to chase,

I should grip hard my teeth, and look where she led,
And brace myself stooping, and give her her head,

And urge her, and soothe her, and serve all her need,
And exult in the thunder and thrill of her speed.

◆

When I Go Home

When I go home, green, green will glow the grass,
Whereon the flight of sun and cloud will pass;
Long lines of wood-ducks through the deepening gloom
Will hold above the west, as wrought on brass,
And fragrant furrows will have delved the loam,
When I go home.

When I go home, the dogwood stars will dash
The solemn woods above the bearded ash,
The yellow-jasmine, whence its vine hath clomb,
Will blaze the valleys with its golden flash,
And every orchard flaunt its polychrome,
When I go home.

When I go home and stroll about the farm,
The thicket and the barnyard will be warm.
Jess will be there, and Nigger Bill, and Tom—
On whom time's chisel works no hint of harm—
And, oh, 'twill be a day to rest and roam,
When I go home!

♦ ♦ ♦

LEONORA MONTERO MARTIN of North Carolina

The Old North State: A Toast

Here's to the land of the Long Leaf Pine,
The Summer Land, where the sun doth shine;
Where the weak grow strong, and the strong grow great—
Here's to "Down Home," the Old North State!

Here's to the land of the cotton blooms white,
Where the scuppernong perfumes the breeze at night,
Where the soft Southern moss and jessamine mate,
Neath the murmuring pines of the Old North State!

Here's to the land where the galax grows,
Where the rhododendron's roseate glows;
Where soars Mount Mitchell's summit great,
In the "Land of the Sky," in the Old North State!

Here's to the land where maidens are fairest,
Where friends are truest, and cold hearts are rarest;
The near land, the dear land, whatever our fate,
The blest land, the best land, the Old North State!

(1904)

♦ ♦ ♦

TURNER MOURING of Arkansas

Song of the Arkansas

I come from Colorado land,
From Rockies and abysses,
From icy streams and coves serene
And jagged precipices.

From canyons deep, where stately ferns
Grow thick on matted hazes,
Where sunbeams tangle in the gloam
Of dark and silent mazes.

I roll through labyrinthian cells,
Through woodlands bleak and hoary,
Through rock-walled mounts with crests of snow
And summits old in story.

Beneath the blue-domed vaulted skies
I stretch my emerald column;
I lift my liquid notes on high,
My anthem sweet and solemn.

And many a field of waving grain
Looks on me as I wander,
And here a farm house quaint and old
And then a city yonder.

And many golden sand-bar planes
Rise on my bosom beaming,
And many an isle with rosy haunts
Blooms in the sunlight gleaming.

I cheer the lovely daffodils,
I kiss the saintly willows;
I make the giant oaks and elms,
Quake 'neath my sounding billows.

Behind the wooded slope I curve,
By brooklet, lake and river;
They join me, and I thunder on
My solemn psalm forever.

♦ ♦ ♦

GEORGE C. STOCKARD

Arkansas

I cannot tell what makes me pine
For those dear native hills of mine;
Nor can I tell why clearer gleams
The water of my mountain streams,
Nor why the earth and sky and air
Seem kindlier there than anywhere.

It must be that by Nature's law
They all belong in Arkansas.
Somehow the twilight's restful hour
Is fullest there of soothing power,
And from the day's soft afterglow,
Heaven can't be very far, I know.
And when the moon beams over all
It seems that I, from joy of soul,
Can almost reach and touch the hem
Of One who walked in Bethlehem.

Far out across the lordly sweep,
Where blue hills in the moonlight sleep,
A twinkling light or tinkling bells
Mark where some rough, plain cotter dwells.
Knock at his door for rest or board,

He meets you like a manor lord.
Feast with him once and you may boast
You sat down with a princely host.
Good faith's a creed and love's a law
In every home in Arkansas.

I love to sit there on the hill,
When all the lights go out and still,
Yet stiller than a tired breast,
Soothed into peace and perfect rest,
The world, a disillusioned waste,
Fills all my soul with visions vast,
And I climb up in Spirit land,
Among the stars, and understand,
Why every fleeting breath I draw,
Seems sweetest here in Arkansas.

♦

War Eagle

Through arbors of vine, where the boughs intertwine,
Thy waters, War Eagle, enchantingly shine;
At morning a feast for the eyes in the east
And at eve the sweet light of repose in the west,
Steals over the glide of thy turbulent tide
And makes thee forever my haven of rest.
To the War Eagle pines from my life's bitter strain,
I oft would return to renew me again;
I could lie down by them and awhile could forget
All the grief I've endured, all the failures I've met.

I could love, I could live, with no wrong to forgive
A fellow and friend to each creature I met.
If fate could provide me a boon more desired
Than a palace whose walls are in splendor attired,
I would ask for the cliff and the high mountain steep
Where the War Eagle waters incessantly leap
At noon to be soothed by the torrent's wild storm,
And at night for its murmur to soothe me to sleep.

♦ ♦ ♦

About the Editor

DR. CLYDE N. WILSON is Emeritus Distinguished Professor of History of the University of South Carolina, where he served from 1971 to 2006. He holds a Ph.D. from the University of North Carolina at Chapel Hill. He recently completed editing of a 28-volume edition of *The Papers of John C. Calhoun* which has received high praise for quality. He is author or editor of more than 40 other books and over 800 articles, essays, and reviews in a variety of books and journals, and has lectured all over the U.S. and in Europe, many of his lectures having been recorded online and on CDs and DVDs. Dr. Wilson directed 17 doctoral dissertations, a number of which have been published. His books written or edited include *Why the South Will Survive, Carolina Cavalier: The Life and Mind of James Johnston Pettigrew, The Essential Calhoun*, three volumes of *The Dictionary of Literary Biography* on American Historians, *From Union to Empire: Essays in the Jeffersonian Tradition, Defending Dixie: Essays in Southern History and Culture, Chronicles of the South, Calhoun: A Statesman for the 21st Century, The Yankee Problem, African American Slavery in Historical Perspective, Looking for Mr. Jefferson*, and *The Land They Loved*, 6 vols. projected. Dr. Wilson is founding director of the Society of Independent Southern Historians; former president of the St. George Tucker Society for Southern Studies; recipient of the Bostick Prize for Contributions to South Carolina Letters, the first annual John Randolph Society Lifetime Achievement Award, and of the Robert E. Lee Medal of the Sons of Confederate Veterans. He is M.E. Bradford Distinguished Professor of the Abbeville Institute; Contributing Editor of *Chronicles: A Magazine of American Culture*; founding dean of the Stephen D. Lee Institute, educational arm of the Sons of Confederate Veterans; and co-founder of Shotwell Publishing.

Dr. Wilson lives in the Dutch Fork of South Carolina, not far from the Santee Swamp where Francis Marion and his men rested between raids on the first invader.

JOE D. HAINES
*The Diary of Col. John Henry Stover Funk
of the Stonewall Brigade, 1861–1862*

CHARLES HAYES
The REAL First Thanksgiving

V.P. HUGHES
Col. John Singleton Mosby: In the News 1862–1916

T.L. HULSEY
25 Texas Heroes

The Constitution of Non-State Government

JOSEPH JAY
*Sacred Conviction:
The South's Stand for Biblical Authority*

JAMES R. KENNEDY
Dixie Rising: Rules for Rebels

*Nullifying Federal and State Gun Control:
A How-To Guide for Gun Owners*

When Rebel Was Cool

*Reconstruction: Destroying the Republic
and Creating an Empire*

Uncle Seth Fought the Yankees: Book 1

WALTER D. KENNEDY
The South's Struggle: America's Hope

Lincoln, The Non-Christian President

Lincoln, Marx, and the GOP

J.R. & W.D. KENNEDY
*Jefferson Davis: High Road to Emancipation
and Constitutional Government*

*Yankee Empire: Aggressive Abroad
and Despotic at Home*

Punished With Poverty: The Suffering South

The South Was Right! 3rd Edition

LEWIS LIBERMAN
Snowflake Buddies; ABC Leftism For Kids!

PHILIP LEIGH
*The Devil's Town: Hot Springs During
The Gangster Era*

U.S. Grant's Failed Presidency

The Causes of the Civil War

*The Dreadful Frauds: Critical Race Theory
and Identity Politics*

JACK MARQUARDT
*Around the World in 80 Years: Confessions
of a Connecticut Confederate*

MICHAEL MARTIN
Southern Grit: Sensing The Siege at Petersburg

SAMUEL MITCHAM
*The Greatest Lynching in American History:
New York, 1863*

*Confederate Patton: Richard Taylor and
The Red River Campaign*

CHARLES T. PACE
Lincoln As He Really Was

*Southern Independence. Why War? The War
To Prevent Southern Independence*

JAMES R. ROESCH
From Founding Fathers To Fire Eaters

KIRKPATRICK SALE
*Emancipation Hell: The Tragedy Wrought
By Lincoln's Emancipation Proclamation*

JOSEPH SCOTCHIE
*The Asheville Connection:
The Making of a Conservative*

*Samuel T. Francis and
Revolution from the Middle*

ANNE W. SMITH
Charlottesville Untold: Inside Unite The Right

Robert E. Lee: A History for Kids

KAREN STOKES
A Legion Of Devils: Sherman In South Carolina

*The Burning of Columbia, S.C.:
A Review of Northern Assertions and Southern Facts*

Carolina Love Letters

*Fortunes of War:
The Adventures of a German Confederate*

*A Confederate in Paris:
Letters of A. Dudley Mann 1867–1879*

Bessie in Love and War

JOSEPH R. STROMBERG
*Southern Story and Song:
Country Music in the 20th Century*

John Taylor of Caroline

Green Altar (Literary Imprint)

CATHARINE SAVAGE BROSMAN
An Aesthetic Education and Other Stories (2nd Ed)

Chained Tree, Chained Owls: Poems

Aerosols and Other Poems

Partial Memoirs

RANDALL IVEY
A New England Romance:
and Other Southern Stories

The Gift of Gab

SUZANNE JOHNSON
Maxcy Gregg's Sporting Journals 1842–1858

JAMES E. KIBLER, JR.
Tiller: Claybank County Series, Vol. 4

The Gentler Gamester

Beyond The Stone: Poems of
Tribute & Remembrance

THOMAS MOORE
A Fatal Mercy:
The Man Who Lost The Civil War

PERRIN LOVETT
The Substitute, Tom Ironsides 1

Judging Athena

KAREN STOKES
Belles
Carolina Twilight
Honor in the Dust
The Immortals
The Soldier's Ghost: A Tale of Charleston

WILLIAM THOMAS
Runaway Haley:
An Imagined Family Saga

The Field of Justice: Moonshine
and Murder in North Georgia

CLYDE N. WILSON
Southern Poets and Poems, 1606 – 1860:
The Land They Loved, Vol. 1

Confederate Poets and Poems, Vol. 1
The Land They Loved, Vol. II

Confederate Poets and Poems, Vol. 2
The Land They Loved, Vol. III

Gold–Bug
(Mystery & Suspense Imprint)

BRANDI PERRY
Splintered: A New Orleans Tale

MARTIN WILSON
To Jekyll and Hide

Free Book Offer